HAZELWOOD

A COMMUNITY STORY

MAY 1, 2023
EDWARD BONNER

Contents

The Beginning   *1*

Belgian Block   *2*

Let the World Go Forth   *3*

Downtown   *4*

Second Avenue   *5*

Old and New   *6*

Glen-Hazel "The Projects"   *7*

Games People Play   *8*

Steps of Hazelwood   *9*

Panther Hollow Lake   *10*

The Pink House   *11*

Lytle Café   *12*

Calvary Cemetery   *13*

Legend of the Razorback   *14*

B-25 Ghost Bomber   *15*

Some Other Experiences   *16*

Hazelwood

Hazelwood, Pittsburgh, Pennsylvania is bordered by Greenfield and Oakland on the north, Squirrel Hill and Glen Hazel on the east, and the Monongahela River.

In 1758, the land was purchased for a little less than $10,000 dollars. It was compromised in agreement with the Native Americans, which was lower than the desirable standards.

Hazelwood takes its name from the hazelnut trees which flourished the land paralleling the Monongahela River. John Woods was among the first settlers that helped survey the town of Pittsburgh. The future boundaries of Pittsburgh included a tract of land called "John Woods Plan." John Woods lived from 1761-1816. The Woods family was a prominent founding family of Pittsburgh. John's father, Colonel George Woods, laid out the plan for the City of Pittsburgh in 1784, and John did the actual drafting. The John Woods house is perhaps the oldest house in the city of Pittsburgh, built in 1792.

John Woods

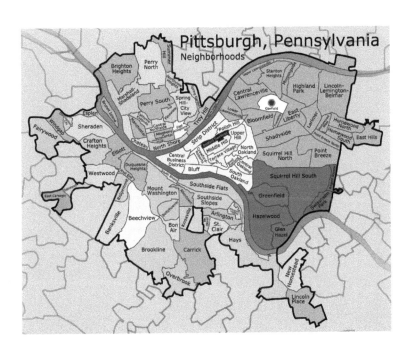

John Woods House

John Woods House

DIED, in Brunswick county, Virginia, on the 16th ult. General JOHN WOODS, of this city, and Member of Congress from this district, in the 55th year of his age ;— a man of transcendant talents in the profession of the law; highly and justly respected for pure integrity and unblemished honour in all his intercourse with the world; and strong in the confidence of his country, from his disinterested, fearless pursuit of what he deemed the public good, regardless of personal consequences to himself.

The manly, elevated cast of his whole character, the zeal, activity and constancy of his friendships and good offices, as well as the urbanity of his manners and the hospitality of his temper, rendered him very dear to all who knew him:—The society in which he lived and held so distinguished a station, universally unites with his immediate relatives in lamenting his premature death.

1

The Beginning

November 28, 1960 is the date I was delivered into this world.
Born in Baltimore Maryland at Saint Agnes Hospital, I weighed a mere
five pounds. Within a year, Rosemary and baby Eddie moved to
Hazelwood and lived with her parents (my grandparents), Rose and
Stanley Rustic. It was a result from a divorce between my parents.
A bustling town that hosted over 200 businesses, Hazelwood was
thriving in the 50's and 60's. It had become home to large Hungarian,
Italian, Slovak, Polish and Irish communities. The Jones and Laughlin
Steel Mill dominated the area. Though the mill did little to enhance the
aesthetics, it was essential for life and employment. In this existence,
Hazelwood was the fountain of life. From a child's heart, our vision
was a divine path aimed for purpose. Some people marveled at the
harvest but not the seed. We were the seed to develop growth in
equality.

My grandparents' home sat on Nansen Street between Flowers Avenue
and Hazelwood Avenue. It was a triplex designed with three houses
attached to each other. It was Similar to today's townhouses or
condominiums. This one block street climbed a towering 28% grade up
to the top meeting with Hazelwood Avenue. Nansen also featured a mix
of 152 sidewalk steps that climbed several feet above the roadway before
leveling out, then continued a step-climb parallel to the hillside.

What happened in my world was an existence manifested into a brilliant adventure. Granted, there were chilling experiences as the sun and moon go down to hell, but the surging impulse was to survive.

My first excursion at four years of age was climbing out my mother's bedroom window onto the front porch roof in my jammies. Early morning, I would shimmy down the drainpipe like a spider descending from its web.

This journey advanced down Nansen Street to Flowers Avenue. Full tilt like a baby duckling, in-toe walking with not one worry in hand. Past Glenwood Avenue and before Gertrude Street, I was searching for my grandmother's friend Elvira. A strange man asked what I was doing and where I lived. In bewilderment, he drove me home. These excursions happened a few times. Another was walking down the same street to see my Uncle Jim working at the fire company at the corner of Flowers and Gertrude. To end this fiasco, my mother tied one of my legs to hers to prevent escaping.

Finger painting the walls matched equivalent design as to Pablo Picasso's mind. A style where everything you can imagine is real. What occurred was spontaneously unexpected. My diaper was empty, and my grandmother hit the floor. Cleaning up was hell.

My first job at five years old was a Barista. "Saturday," six in the morning I decided to make coffee for my grandfather. Not knowing what I was doing, I poured the grinds down the kitchen sink. Well, let's say about an inch of water laid stagnant on the kitchen floor. Another chore for my grandparents.

One of the most painful episodes in my life was taking a bath in a large metal washtub. I was left alone in the cellar. Having a splendid time playing, I looked over the edge and noticed a blue jar setting on the floor. Curious, I opened the jar in the tub. As a result, my body was covered in blue paint. Frantic, I saw a gallon can of turpentine. Needless to say, every part of my body burned. I felt like a flaming candle glowing in the night. Time was the only cure that relieved the pain.

Where was my beautiful mother at the time? Well, she worked at a beauty salon on Murray Avenue in the Squirrel Hill section of Pittsburgh between Lilac Street and Loretta Street. She worked as a beautician. Occasionally, my grandfather would drive me to visit her, and I would get my hair cut for free. It was great to see her working. Most of the time I wouldn't see my mother until bedtime or when she was off.

On her days off, we would take a trip to Frick Park. It was one of Henry Clay Frick's donations to Pittsburgh. Opened in 1927, 151 acres of beautiful woodlands and the famous blue slide playground, where kids flocked from all over the city to play. I can still see myself flying down that concrete slide and ending on the rubber tarmac. Rushing off to climb the steps and fly down again. What a blast!

Most recently, 106 acres were developed as part of a layout that created the Summerset at Frick Park and restored the Nine Mile Run stream valley. Today, Frick Park stretches from its northern borders in Point Breeze down to the Monongahela River.

Some days my grandparents would take me to the Calvary Cemetery where my great grandmother "Maria" is buried. Maria's maiden name was Bevilacqua, and yes, she was a relative to American Cardinal Anthony Bevilacqua. He was the former Bishop of Pittsburgh and Archbishop of Philadelphia. In 1886, the diocese established the Calvary Cemetery Association and Calvary Cemetery, a 200-acre tract of land in the Hazelwood area of Pittsburgh. The first burial took place in June 1888. Calvary Cemetery remains the largest of the diocesan cemeteries.

What's unique about going to my great grandmother's plot was the view looking down the mountain side to Homestead and the High-Level Bridge "Grays Bridge." The sight was amazing, especially for a young child. Homestead Works of U. S. Steel, which at one time produced nearly a third of all steel used in the United States was a fire breathing monster. The mill ran parallel with the Monongahela River. Smoke belched in a distant foreground, trains moved to and from.

But from this mountain high, sound was silent. A peaceful serenity filled your thoughts. A gentle breeze wafted the scent of fresh flowers in the air.

My grandfather Stanley, was employed at US Steel/ Edgar Thomson Works in Braddock Pennsylvania. The town was named after General Edward Braddock, the British officer and commander for the Thirteen Colonies during the start of the French and Indian war. Known for his disastrous expedition against the French in 1755 which he lost his life.

Every Saturday morning, I would travel with my grandfather to Braddock. He would stop at work to get his paycheck and schedule. Later we would go to the local beer garden. "Dad" as I called him, would have a couple beers and I sat in a booth eating pickled eggs.
Once in a while I would see him play the numbers. Later we would stop at the local bakery to pick up some donuts. These donuts were unusual. Old fashion donuts on a stick, an amazing treat served warm and golden.

Driving home we would go across the Rankin Bridge. The road before the bridge was like a circle to merge on. Down Braddock Ave, going into Kenmar Ave, Making a right on Carrie Furnace Blvd. Then around to meet South Braddock Ave. finally, the Rankin Bridge. At the end of the bridge, we would make a right turn onto route 837 through Homestead.

Driving through town you would see the US Steel's Homestead works. The 19th-century steel plant helped make Pittsburgh the greatest Steel City in America. The steel mill is also known for the "Homestead Steel Strike, or the Homestead Massacre." The company workers had an industrial lockout that erupted into a strike on July 1, 1892. It climaxed into a battle between the strikers and a private security firm known as the Pinkertons on July 6, 1892. Nine strikers and seven Pinkertons were killed; many strikers and most of the remaining Pinkertons were injured, some seriously. The sheriff unable to recruit local residents against the strikers, appealed to Governor William Stone for support; eight thousand militia arrived killing many people.

One evening my grandfather and I were sitting on the back porch gazing at the sky. I asked him a question. "Why was there an orange glow?" His answer. "If you ever see that orange glow disappear, there will be many jobs lost." At six years old, I did not understand, but today I see the hardship of his meaning.

Jones and Laughlin Steel company built plants on both sides of the Monongahela River. The operations on the South Side and Hazelwood became the industrial core. During the peak industry, J & L employed close to 12,000 workers and Hazelwood grew to 13,000 multicultural residents.

A magnificent power combined with fearless men and women molded Pittsburgh as awe-inspiring workhorse. Molten steel pouring from gigantic hearths, relentless pounding of pure ingots rolled into beams then cooled to a tempered iron. Everything was big, dangerous and filthy. Day and night towering smokestacks funneled the smell of rotten eggs into the air. The mills never shut down, "twenty-four seven." Years of prosperity and promises fulfilled thousands of dreams.

Another major employer in Hazelwood was the Baltimore & Ohio Railroad, "B&O." The community was divided between the railroaders and the millworkers. The railroaders lived in Glenwood and the millworkers lived in Hazelwood. In 1974 J & L was purchased by Ling-Temco-Vought Incorporation "LTV".
Twenty years later, the plants closed and ceased operation.

Within a couple years, my grandparent's living room transformed into my bedroom. That's when the word "freedom" had a twist. Early in the morning, I would venture behind the house to the woods. Known today as O.W.L. Hollow. For me it was just the woods. These woods spanned from Nansen St. all the way to Monongahela St. across from the Pittsburgh Bureau of Fire | 13 Engine & Truck.

Climbing trees, building shacks, catching critters was my day. Something unusual to have your own getaway within a concrete jungle. Except the one incident that is haunting my brain.
"Playing With Matches." A strike, a light, a burn. Burning sticks were intriguing for a kid, until one spark caused hell. There was an old automobile bench seat tossed into the hollow. I guess the older kids would sit and party. Well, the seat ignited like a flaming torch. I bolted home to get a bucket of water. Slipping and falling on the ground became inevitable. A single spark caused one of the most severe fires in Hazelwood with no casualties. Luckily only the woods caught fire.
I hid under the couch for hours until my grandmother found me.
Thinking I was going to jail, I blamed this kid. The last time I saw the boy was when his mother was beating his ass walking up Nansen Street. That was the end of experimenting with matches.

Nansen Street amounted to a thrill for automobiles, bicycles and runners. You may add "heart attack hill" for climbing the steps parallel to the road.

The experience driving down Nansen Street was quiet and amazingly exciting, especially when you are a passenger. The view is a tunnel-vision mania. A few times it may feel like everyone is just going to fall forward and out in front of the car, but it won't happen. The potholes make it extremely amusing. Shifting the gears from "3", "2" , or "L" , was important for an ease at controlling your car's speed and and to save wear on your brakes. At that time, seatbelts were not required until 1968.

With a one speed gear on your bike, bicycling was a rare sight. Very few would ride up or down Nansen Street. Frequently you would see people walking their bikes up or down the hill for fear of falling.

Winter storms took over Hazelwood, giving kids the chance to spend days sled riding on a fresh layer of snow. Nansen Street was a well-known hill for this purpose. As soon as the snow fell, Nansen Street was nearly impossible to drive on. People of all ages brought sleds, cardboard boxes and aluminum flying saucer sleds. A ramp would be built at bottom of the hill making the sled rider airborne. The majority of kids would begin sledding in the middle of the hill for safety reasons, only the fearless started from the top, which was Hazelwood Avenue. Sledding from this area was and still is dangerous due to the parked cars and heavy traffic perpendicular to the street. Few have crashed under a parked car or sparked across Flowers Avenue. Luckily no one was injured severely. Riding like a double decker bus, I was sledding at night with my best friend, and we slid under a parked car. I still have the scars on my head.

Nansen Street

2

Belgian Block

There is a lot of confusion about "cobblestone" and "Belgian block." Many people assume that they refer to types of rock, like granite or marble. Some people think Belgian blocks were quarried in Belgium -- you know, like French Fries in France. Actually, the French Fry is unequivocally Belgian."
The Belgian block refers not to the type of stone, but the way it is cut in rectangles. People often refer to roads paved this way as "cobblestone streets," but that isn't exactly correct.
Cobblestones are rounded, typically because they've been worn smooth by rivers. They might be hell to drive on, but they were cheap to use. You could just dredge them up from the river and fabricate a road or path.

Hazelwood Avenue was a unique road to travel. Constructed of Belgian blocks made it an interesting ride. First there is an uphill climb from Beechwood Boulevard and past the main entrance of the Calvary Cemetery which is at the crest of the hill. The street then descends at a gentle manageable grade, then flattens out somewhat near the Gladstone Junior High baseball field (Oil Field) before another gentle descent. After negotiating a small blind turn, the street falls abruptly parallel to Gladstone Junior High and finally ends across Second Avenue "below the tracks." Only visitors and angels loved the Belgian blocks. The rest of us, those who have to traveled by foot or wheel every day, detested them, feared them…or admired them from a yonder.

Belgium Block

With wear, the blocks eventually transforms into a smooth slithery street. They can be slippery in the rain, treacherous if you are on a bicycle. When it snows,each block resembles an ice cube and ugliness yields its new name.

Car wheels make a drumming sound that adds to the hustle and bustle of the town. The bumps battle and rattle your brain. When it is dark and raining, every block catches a gleaming streetlight. The road is like a path of pearls. Take it slow and enjoy the beauty.

Looking back in history. There was a local hero by the name of John Minadeo. John was a young man from the Hazelwood area, and a son of Italian immigrants in the 1950s. While patrolling as a student crossing guard for Gladstone Elementary School, John Minadeo was at his post on the corner of Hazelwood Avenue and Second Avenue. A car at the top of Hazelwood Avenue lost its brakes and barreled down the hill. The driver trying to avoid another automobile at the intersection of Hazelwood and Second Avenue, veered his car to the right causing it to vault onto the sidewalk straight and into a group of school children. John Minadeo in an effort pushed aside a number of children just before the rampant car crashed into him. John's actions that day saved four students. Unfortunately, the crash seized the lives of John Minadeo and classmate Ella Cornelius. Over 7,000 people attended John Minadeo's funeral.

Mayor David L. Lawrence recognized John Minadeo's bravery, and in 1956, then-Vice President Richard Nixon awarded Minadeo a lifesaving commendation. In 1957, Minadeo Elementary School was opened in Squirrel Hill on behalf of John Minadeo's sacrifice. John was only 17 years old.

Going back in time, the famous Glenwood Bridge was built over the Monongahela River in 1894. The Glenwood Bridge was an iron bridge with a wooden deck which carried streetcars and automobiles across the river. The route for the trolleys was between Pittsburgh and Homestead. As a result, the line went through Hazelwood.

The few times going across the bridge with my mother in her Ford Falcon automobile, I remember the holes in the wooden planks and the rickety sounds that echoed in your ears. Ten miles per hour was the maximum speed for crossing this bridge. Thrilling and frightening was an amusement ride on its own, especially when you would see the river below. What made it more interesting, my mother's car had a hole in the passengers' floor, all the better to see. Squeaky, clickety, clank!!! The old decaying bridge was replaced with a brand-new cantilever bridge.

3

Let The World Go Forth

The year 1968 remains one of the most turbulent single years in world history. Historical achievements, shocking assassinations and a much appalling war bled through countries all over the world. The early age of television brought these events into our living room to experience live broadcasting venues.

The Vietnam War was a long controversial conflict that marked North Vietnam "communist government" against South Vietnam and its prominent ally the United States. More than 58,000 Americans were killed in the Vietnam War. The media coverage brought the horrors of war into our homes. As an eight-year-old watching the news with your grandfather, scenes of combat soldiers shooting into the jungle were uncomprehensive. Ugly, cruel in a stalemate war, the wounded are shown being carried off into helicopters. Naked children are crying for their parents. War is now imbedded into the eyes of a young lad, never to be forgotten.

I was attending Saint Stephens school when a classmate's brother was killed in Vietnam. "Tragedy has finally echoed in our town."
I remember the day our second-grade class walked down Elizabeth Streetto the O'Connor Funeral home on Second Avenue.
There was an overwhelming sense of dread not knowing what to say or how to act at a funeral home. Walking through a long hallway with viewing rooms on both sides had a startling effect on the mind.

All five senses come into play in a funeral home.
Smell has a more powerful impact than thought. Floral arrangements were displayed, candles and incense helped create a meaningful experience for each student.

Sight was one of the most compelling senses, as there was so much to take in. The funeral displays beautiful flowers, grieving people and finally the deceased. Fortunately, his casket was closed. Only his photo and medals were displayed for all the mourners to view.

A faint sound was heard in the background. Music provided a meaningful wisdom to each living soul. Sympathy, sharing memories. and crying was an unforgettable experience.

Hugging loved ones, touching memorabilia displays are all important for comforting those in grief. This is a beginning experience for healing.

Taste: snacks, desserts and beverages may calm the emotional level to have the best memories of a loved one. Our class did not stay for the snacks. Overall, I hate funerals. My mother always said: "Never go straight home from a funeral home, it's bad luck. Stop and get a coffee."

The beginning of a new generation has taken over the United States. A division of violence and dismay within our society erupted when civil rights leader Dr. Martin Luther King Jr. was assassinated on April 4,1968 by fugitive # 277 James Earl Ray, a man on the FBI's most wanted list. In 1967 James Earl Ray escaped from the Missouri State Penitentiary by hiding in a bread truck from the prison bakery.

On the day Dr. King was assassinated, James Earl Ray acquired a room in a boarding house that had a view to the Lorraine Motel in Memphis, Tennessee. At the time of the assassination, Dr. King was on the second-floor balcony of the Lorraine Motel, on Mulberry Street between Hulin Avenue and E. Butler Avenue, where he had been staying while in Memphis to support a strike by the City of Memphis sanitation workers. Dr. King was shot by a .30-06 rifle bullet that hit the jaw and traveled through his neck severing his spinal cord. He was taken to St. Joseph's hospital near Memphis. At 7:05 p. m. Dr. Martin Luther King Jr. was pronounced dead. He was only 39 years old.

I clearly remember the major outbreaks of violence that was a result from Dr. King's death. Riots, looting, firebombing in over 100 American cities.

In Hazelwood, families had to board up their windows.
On Second Avenue, store front windows were smashed, and businesses looted. While attending St. Stephen's school, protestors were lined up outside on the corner of E. Elizabeth Street and Glenwood Avenue. Police were sent to escort students from school to their parent's car. To understand the thoughts of a young child, I drafted a poem about feelings.

HORROR

Reality
Boarded windows and doors.
Black and white force marked unambiguous from a significant distance.

Escorted from schools,
They are lined up watching.
Ready to thrash the innocence of society.

One distinguished and honored human
assassinated,
terminated with extreme violence.

Stabbings go unnoticed on the streets, in the bars and in schools.

With the sound of sirens, the night sky glows a reddish color high in the night sky.

A young boy cannot understand the word hate.
Why in this beautiful world made from God's hands,
is being destroyed?

We were born to love and love back.
Born as nature feeds this world to survive.

Shortly after Martin Luther King's assassination, on April 23, 1968, students for a Democratic Society and Students for the Afro-American Society began a nonviolent occupation of campus buildings that lasted nearly a week at Columbia University in New York City. Students and local supporters called for the university to end research for the Vietnam war and to end construction of a gym in Morningside Park. Segregation was the primary grounds for the production of the gym.

After negotiations failed, the school administration sent in the police to remove the students. As a result, many of the students were injured and over 700 arrested. Demonstrations in April ensued violent demonstrations in May, and then a student strike. As a result, the university did not build the gym and renounced its membership in the Institute for Defense Analysis.

"Now how does an eight-year-old remember all this?" I only remember what I observed on the television.

June 5 was a continuation of tragic events in 1968. On the night of the California primary for the Democratic presidential nomination, senator Robert F. Kennedy was leaving the Ambassador Hotel in Los Angeles when he was shot by a Jordanian immigrant "Sirhan Sirhan." Sirhan was carrying a .22 caliber handgun rolled up in a campaign poster. Kennedy was exiting through the kitchen when Sirhan shot Kennedy three times, with one lethal bullet entering his head. Seeing this shooting captured on the news was a horrendous image transmitted around the world. On my grandparents black and white television, I could see a man holding Robert Kennedy's head up off the ground. Robert's lips were. moving as if he was talking. People were screaming and crying in the background. Such a violent act that many could not comprehend.

After a two-month long manhunt, James Earl Ray was captured on June 8, 1968, at London's Heathrow Airport. On March 10, 1969, Ray pleaded guilty to the murder of Martin Luther King Junior. Ray was sentenced to 99 years. Later that same year, Ray escaped with six other convicts. He was recaptured three days later and given a 100-year sentence. James Earl Ray died April 23, 1998. As of today, King's family are unanimous on one key point: James Earl Ray did not kill Martin Luther King.

Martin Luther King Jr.

Robert Francis Kennedy

The 1968 Summer Olympics, known as the XIX Olympiad, was an international multi-sport event held from 12th to 27th October 1968 in Mexico City, Mexico.

One of my all-time favorites was George Foreman, who won the gold medal in the heavyweight boxing division by defeating Soviet Ionas Chepulis in the second-round with a TKO. After the victory, Foreman waved a small American flag as he bowed to the crowd.

Watching the Olympics was exciting. I love sports and all sports. One day two U. S. Olympic athletes raised their fists on the podium while playing the Star-Spangled Banner. Tommie Smith won the gold medal and John Carlos won the bronze medal. They used their medal wins as an opportunity to focus on the social issues heating up in the United States. The Civil Rights movement was at an escalated height, and racial hostilities sought for equal freedom. Carlos and Smith appeared on the podium wearing black socks without shoes to bring attention to the poverty in the African American communities and for the oppressed people around the world.

Peter Norman was the silver medal winner from Australia. Peter did not raise his fist, but also gave support for Carlos and Smith. Peter was from a working-class family in Melbourne, Australia. A compassionate family, they volunteered much of their time to the Salvation Army. Part of their faith was the belief that all men were created equal. At that time, Australia was experiencing racial tension of its own. Because of Norman's support for equality, he was severely punished by the Australian sports association. In the years proceeding, Peter posted the fastest time in the qualifiers for the Olympic team. He was excluded in the 1972 Olympics. Immediately he retired from the sport, suffered from depression, alcoholism and painkiller addiction. He was said to use his silver medal as a doorstop.

Peter Norman

Tommie Smith

John Carlos

On a cold Monday morning, February 17, 1969. Pandemonium hit Gladstone High School in Hazelwood. Fights in hallways created a "panic situation." Many students in attendance had fled the school. Classes resumed after school officials and police calmed things down, but teachers stood before rooms with empty desks. Uniformed police continued to roam the hallways and grounds to control violence.

Beginning the next day in class, everything was relatively calm. However, near its end, knives flashed in a stairway outside the school entrance. Two teenage boys who lived a half-mile apart dueled with blades. Blood spattered on the tile floor. Both students were transported to local hospitals. Once again, police armed with batons arrived at the school. This time, they made arrests. Students were told to stay in their classrooms. Officials hoped to prevent a mass evacuation. At one point, police escorted two girls from the building and were pelted with bottles thrown from a second-floor window.

On November 5th, 1969, Richard Nixon won the presidency of theUnited States. Nixon played a smart role in this election as he called on the "silent majority." This was a process to get the Conservative voters who did not participate in public policy. A process that Ronald Reagan and Donald Trump would follow. Richard Nixon pledged that the UnitedStates would continue to support the Vietnam War until the communists agreed to a peaceful ending. With the anti-war and civil rights protest, Nixon promised to bring the U.S. citizens together again.

When I was in third grade at St. Stephens School, we had an in-school election for the presidencies. I volunteered to campaign for Nixon and Diane volunteered for Hubert Humphrey. We went to each classroom to promote Nixon and Humphrey for President. We had posters, buttons and pencils. Red pencil with "Nixon" and blue buttons for "Humphrey." Our speech was plain and fast. The reason I volunteered was to get out of class. This was my first taste at BS.

Hazelwood had many stores; 2 supermarkets, 4 gas stations, banks, a 5 &10 store and Fisher's drug store on the corner of Flowers and 2nd Ave. Islay's Ice Cream and over 200 storefronts lined 2nd Ave. Huckster food trucks and milk trucks clanged and rambled weekly in the neighborhoods.

Cutting through backyards and alleys to get home was no issue.

We cleaned and collected pop/soda bottles, two cents refund for each bottle. Everyone would speak like they knew you and call your parents if you did something wrong. We feared getting paddled by the principal. We didn't have bullying. We took care of the troublemakers ourselves.

We played outside in every seasonal condition. All we needed was a ball, bat, glove, skates, bike, hockey stick and whatever to keep us busy. We played hide and seek, tag, street football, baseball, basketball, soccer and street hockey. We were not afraid of anything except dogs and rats. Rats as big as cats with which you didn't fool around with. The "streetlights" were our curfew call, and parental screams could be heard throughout the neighborhood to get your "ass" home.

Day of the Bully

Clear as a shattered glass across my face

The backyard bully driven down in his place

Street football is a sport of its own

Local neighborhoods play for the throne

This story is one of kind

No one will understand the thought behind

School bully walks in at bay

I motion to my buddy

There's the kid at class

Pretentious, intimidates and imbalance

What an ass

As he pushes his way

My friend whispers in my ear

Let's tackle him to the ground

Acknowledge and willing

We knocked him silly

Hold him down my comrade blurts out

What do we do now

I scream and shout

Hold him

Do you want him to despise and make your class cry

I said no

Unknowing and shocking

He pulls his zipper down and pissed on his head

At first, I was happy as hell

Then my emotion fell

I let him go

He ran home

Never again a bully

The average age for girls to begin puberty is 11, while for boys is age 12. However, it can be normal for puberty to begin from ages of 8 to 14. Diane; our third-grade crush, only she didn't know. One day my friend Donald and I concocted the most ingenious operation in third grade history. "At least for us." Every day at recess, Diane would be the first student to flop back into her seat. She would be the only student in the classroom at this time. While the teacher Mrs. Duffy would be watching the students in the hall, Donald and I decided to give Diane a kiss. Yes! A freaking Kiss. We had to be alert and act fast. Friday morning at nine was our first recess, it was time. Like James Bond, secret agent working for M16 who answers to his codename "007" . Diane sat in the third seat, first row. The remainder of the students were playing games in the hall. They had about five minutes left before returning into the classroom. Dashing in, I sat on Diane's lap and gave her a kiss. Five seconds later, Donald followed and duplicated this extraordinary act of excitement. Running back to our own desk, the class started returning from recess. Half an hour into class, Mrs. Duffy made a speech about certain things that should not be done in class. She never mentioned our names, only a little stare at Donald and me.

July 20th 1969 marked man's first step on the moon. A new era in history has prevailed when the lunar module "Eagle" gently settled on the dusty surface of serenity. Neil Armstrong, Buzz Aldrin and Michael Collins became the first crew to successfully land on the Moon.

Armstrong's famous quoted, "One Small Step for Man, One Giant Leap for Mankind" will never be forgotten. Armstrong and his crew are referred to as pathfinders in history. When taking the first steps on the Moon's surface, Armstrong was shown live on a global television broadcast that was watched by over 600 million people. Everyone was screaming outside. Fireworks were heard all over Pittsburgh. What a special day for me to witness this extraordinary achievement.

4

Downtown

Around 1969, my mother started working at the Kaufman's department store in Pittsburgh. She worked on the twelfth floor which was called the Adoria Beauty Salon. Throughout the twelfthfloor each salon chair was evenly placed with a wash basin. One of my mother's clients was Mrs. Kaufman. I would always ask what she was like. "Very polite," my mother would say. Many famous people had their hair cut or styled at the beauty salon. One woman was Elizabeth Taylor. Elizabeth Taylor would show up unexpectedly to have her hair styled.
Kaufman's was located at 5th Avenue and Smithfield Street.
The famous Kaufman's clock suspended on the corner of the building, was a meeting place for friends.
"Meet me under the Kaufman's clock," was the customary saying.
One may encounter groups of golden robed monks with shaved heads and thin ponytails chanting under the Kaufman's clock.
"The Hare Krishna." Hare Krishna first appeared in public at anti-war demonstrations and counterculture events in the late 1960s. This was the age when western religions were being given the boot. The war in Vietnam had not only caused many to rethink their patriotism to the country but the influential traditions to God. Krishna was easy to sell to hippies. Most of them abandon religion when they rejected their parents. Hippies did not want to hear about death. Death was a calamity. Krishna was cool. They played the flute and hung out with beautiful girls. They wore flowers and feathers and went barefoot… Seeing the bald-headed Hare Krishna dancing, chanting and playing with their finger cymbals. I wanted nothing to do with it.

Meet me under the Kaufman's clock

One of my favorite holiday memories downtown was a visit to the animated windows of the city's department stores. A beginning once defined the Christmas season through the 1980s. Kaufmann's, Joseph Horne Company, Gimbels, competed intensely to unveil their showpiece windows of the year. Winning this festive battle carried high stakes. The windows enticed customers to each store's celebration. "Toyland" and a talk with Santa, generated important roles for the holiday season. Each became a cherished part of what it meant to be a Pittsburgher at Christmas time. Fantastic themes and mechanical animation provided continuous excitement for many children and adults. Department stores provided visions of Santa with children's stories and fairy tales such as "Alice in Wonderland," "Cinderella," and "Goldilocks and the Three Bears."

Exploring Pittsburgh's market square was a true charm in the heart of city. Originally named "Diamond Way" in colonial times and Market Street, the square was home to the first courthouse, first jail "both in 1795" and the first newspaper the Pittsburgh Gazette "1786". Goods were shipped to the city by steamboat to the Mon Wharf and brought to the square. Farmers sold produce and merchants sold their wares.
As the city grew and expanded, the courthouse moved to Grant Street and the square became exclusively a market district.
What I remember about Market Street was the smell. Some good, some bad. I was always with my grandmother shopping. The street was very diverse with produce and poultry. Whether it was fresh fruit or hanging plucked chickens. Market Street enjoyed a steady stream of people looking for something to put on the dinner table.

Recalling Pittsburgh's movie theater legacy recollects the fun and excitement for all film fanatics. It seemed there was a movie theater at every block, a multicultural array of advents every day. For first run movies, the Gateway Theater was your choice. At such an early age, I can remember going to the Gateway Theater to see Mary Poppins and the Sound of Music. An army of people would wait in line to purchase tickets. The Gateway Theater was located on Sixth Street, now the city'scultural district. In 1942 it was the world's first nickelodeon to open.

Another beautiful palace theater was the Warner. Located on Fifth Avenue, the theater's interior was primarily beige with deep red carpeting and curtains. Its large marquee posted huge mylars on its side, depicting the poster artwork for the current film. This made the theater a special focus in the downtown center, especially at night. Like a castle, the auditorium had a huge basement with spiral steps made out of stone. The basement had markings on the wall giving the water level of the 1937 St. Patrick's Day flood in Pittsburgh. It was also a "Fall Out Shelter" with food supplies and water containers.

The Pittsburgh rock scene produced many nationally known artists and many memorable recordings beginning in the early 1960s. One well known theater called the Stanley Theater was located on Seventh and Penn. This great place had musical performers like the Grateful Dead, David Bowie, Yes, King Crimson, and Bob Seger. The Stanley hosted concerts each week by top rock, jazz, country, and R&B artists and also presented touring Broadway musicals. Billboard Magazine named the Stanley Theater the "Number One Auditorium in the U.S." several times throughout the 1970s and 1980s. Pittsburgh continues to be a vital cultural mecca producing new musicians for the world.

At nine years old, twenty cents was the price to ride on the Port Authority Transit (Pat) bus from Hazelwood to downtown Pittsburgh. On weekends, I'd walk down Flowers Avenue to Second Avenue, then take the Pat bus to town and get dropped off in front of Kaufman's. I would surprise my mother at work by spending a little time with her and maybe get a haircut. After my visit, I would walk to the Fiesta movie theater and see a matinee. Before going home, Jenkins Arcade was my last stop. It was a unique building with a multiplicity of shops. The Jenkins Arcade was the first indoor shopping mall in the United States.

Jenkins Arcade

5

Second Avenue

The G.C. Murphy's Five and Ten located at Second Ave. and Flowers Ave., sold general merchandise, such as apparel, automotive parts, dry goods, hardware, home furnishings, and a selection of groceries. It usually sold them at discounted prices, sometimes at one or several fixed price points, such as one dollar, or historically, five and ten cents. The Five and Ten store reminds me of today's Target, Walmart and Dollar stores combined. The isles were narrow and the shelves full of products above your head. The place smelled musty and the wood floor creaked with each walking step. Some shelves were full of penny candy, enough to rot all your teeth in a month.

Across Flowers Ave. from Five and Ten was Fisher's Drug store. Fisher's had the "modern" counter and cast-iron porcelain fountain parlor bar stools. The original Cherry Coke was a favorite. "Coke with grenadine syrup." Let us not forget the famous "Shirley Temple" drink. Ginger ale mixed with a splash of grenadine, garnished with a maraschino cherry. These simple drinks made a kid smile from ear to ear. The only problem with Fisher's Drug store was Mr. Fisher. He sat at the end of the counter, with the meanest look on his face watching everyone. Mr. Fisher had only one leg and walked with one crutch under his arm. I wonder what happened to him.

Dimperio's, one of the neighborhood's last remaining grocery stores, closed in 2008 after almost 80 years due to several robbery attempts and incessant shoplifting. Was a favorite to shop. I found out recently that Dimperio was related to a Galuppo. Galuppo is related to my great grandparents and also comes up owner of Dimperio's.

In the 1950's, a few police officers would walk the beat in Hazelwood. One well known police officer named Joe Palmer, maintained law and order from Hazelwood to Glenwood. Officer Joe Palmer would stroll down Second Avenue and check every business on what was then a bustling stretch of stores and saloons. It was a mile long beat from Hazelwood Avenue to the Glenwood Bridge.
During the school year, Officer Palmer would ask the children how they were performing in class. He would give the kids a surprise for every "A" they earned on their report cards.

At one time there were 38 bars between Hazelwood Avenue and the Glenwood Bridge, and they were not all on Second Avenue.
The State Liquor Store was across Second Avenue from Islay's.
The Hazelwood Bank was bankrolled by many local businessmen.

There were four drugstores, three bowling alleys, two movie theaters, two furniture stores, two bakeries (Retenauer's was one).
The neighborhood had four supermarkets, A&P, Kroger, Dimperio's, the AZ Market and probably another below the tracks.
Also, there were several clubs, Kiwanis, American Legion, Moose, and the Hungarians. A Murphy's 5& 10 was present in the community as well.

5 & 10 Store

Fisher's Drug Store

Dimperio's Market

Everyone shopped at
Demperio's for groceries

In the early 1930's, Islay's dairy company moved into the Pittsburgh area to sell farm-fresh products and a wide variety of deli meats, cheeses and ice cream. A tradition was born in Pittsburgh as families streamed in on a sizzling summer day for the "Skyscraper" cones,butter, cheese and Islay's signature Chipped Chopped Ham and Old Fashioned Ice Cream. The original Klondike bar created by Islay's was handmade and dipped into rich delicious Swiss milk chocolate.

In Hazelwood, Islay's was located on Second Avenue across from the G. C. Murphy's 5 & 10 store and down from Grercio's Vegetables. Opened till 12 midnight, Islay's was a teenage hangout on weekends. Islay's had a big old fashioned pickle barrel where you could buy huge dill pickles and they would wrap them in wax paper for you to hold just like a cone. The hand-dipped ice cream, banana splits, sundaes and the fabulous shakes that went with the juicy burgers & hot fries made your mouth water. Each table had an individual jukebox. It was so much fun pushing the buttons, we drove our parents crazy always asking for a nickel or dime to play a song.

Sharing of Islay's and other memories from my classmates growing up in Hazelwood:

Cathy DiThomas Farkal
The grand memory I have is when my mom would walk me and my little sister and brother down to get an ice cream cone which was always a real treat!

Renee Marino
My father would take us to Isaly's for lunch meat and if I were lucky he would treat me to a square bar of Vanilla ice-cream covered in chocolate.

David King
I remember walking to Isaly's and getting a Chipped Ham sandwich and ice cream cone with my mom. I loved the giant pickles.I could barely hold them in my hands.

David North

It was so cool when they had the Klondike's with the pink center. If you were LUCKY, that meant you won a free pack of Klondike's!!!

Joe Szewcow

I remember going in and asking for a milkshake. I would watch the lady scoops out the ice cream and plops a few scoops into the tall silvermetallic cup. Then she would pour in some milk, and then place the silver cup on the green machine and turn it on.
I could hear the yummy concoction mixing. After a bit of time, which seemed like forever to an 8-year-old, she would pour the mixture into aglass and stick a straw into it. I would thank her and enjoy my treat.
A unique sound that machine made while mixing up the ingredients of that milkshake. Can still hear it now. Thanks for the trip down memory lane.

Valerie Ondruseck

Well, the movie house would show triple scary movies. Sundays after church, Urs and I would go to corner drug store for banana splits at the soda fountain. Pretty much everyone did. Great memories of growing up in Hazelwood. We would all play ball games on our street.

Francis Iannotta

I grew up on Flowers Avenue. Consequently, as a child, I'd frequently stop a Perhac's on my way from playing ball on the Oil Field to stock up on penny candy and pop. Mr. Perhac was a dear man with patience of a saint. I can still envision him with his apron and cap, standing behind that candy counter while I decided which items to purchase with my quarter.

Tom Hutchison

My grandmother told us of train tracks up and down East Elizabeth St. where mules would pull coal cars from the prairie and the woods to Second Avenue.

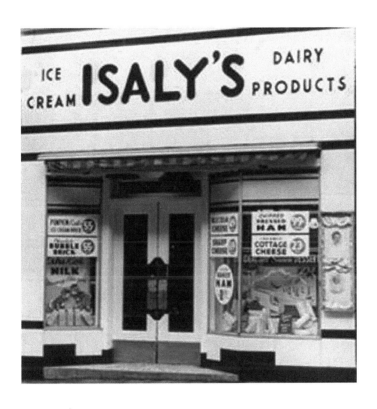

Hazelwood Theater——4921 Second Avenue

When the steel industry was at its height in Pittsburgh, many neighborhoods like Hazelwood could support their own movie theaters. On many days during this era. The Hazelwood Theater was a popular entertainment site for many in the community. Listed in the almanac as the New Hazelwood Theater, the owner was Nathan Landy, who also owned the Grand and New McKee in Pittsburgh as well as the Paramount in Braddock. The last listing for films in The Pittsburgh Press is the week of April 11-17, 1962, with "The Minotaur." Seventeen cartoons on Saturday. It cost 22 cents to get in. Of course, my memory of the theater was only the building closed for demolishing.

Second Avenue was lined with many familiar names of the times including. Hazelwood Hardware, John Carusos Bar and Café, Levin and Son Appliances, Dave Shoes, Kerrs Flowers, Brims, A & P grocery store, and so forth. One memory that remains in my mind was seeing the aftermath of an accident on Second Avenue (Irvine St.) and Berwick St.

SECOND AVENUE

1969
A memory so strong I can hear the cries and pain
7 am. Rise and shine
A dazzling summer morning for a day of fishing at Panther Hollow
The walk is far: 3 miles or more

Down Flowers and Second Avenue

Arriving early at the boat house to receive a free bamboo pole for the day
A 10 foot line tied with a shiny hook

Gorgeous and graceful
As the rolling waves flow beneath the golden sun
Adds memories of laughter and fun

Shade creeps over the lake
Hours seem like minutes

4 pm

Time for me to make haste

The walk feels long; my body tired
I didn't care; I had a perfect day

Second Avenue was booming
Traffic at full force
People driving from a long day at work

Not knowing the tragedy that lies ahead

I start running to get home for dinner and bed

As I reach the small crest of a hill

Two ladies lay on the road
One sitting up moaning; In her bare feet
The other woman; lay lifeless on the ground

Their shopping bags thrown
Food all over the road
And shoes empty of bodies
from the ladies that lay

Off to the side was a car that hit a pole
The man still inside

As I walk a few feet away
Moaning
I hear moaning and moaning

No cries

Only
Pain from this woman sitting on the ground

I walk by this woman

Ten feet away
I wasn't even 9, a young boy astray

I saw dark red puddles on the road
Skid marks from tires
The smell of burning rubber

When I got home, I did not say a word. I was too scared
Only later that week
I found out the women died at the scene

I swear her body covers me
Moaning of pain

Today, I see no face
Only the moaning
That haunts my soul
I will never forget my last
Walk on Second Avenue
I can hear her screaming!

Traveling north down Second Avenue, I encountered the old Elizabeth Pharmacy sitting at the corner of Second Ave. and Elizabeth Street. Since 1910 at 5041 Second Ave., this old-fashioned general store provided just about anything for their customers. The pharmacy supplies avariety of goods from food and toys to household items.

The bright blue and yellow exterior is a flashy display for the community to enjoy.

At one time, next to Elizabeth Pharmacy, sat Mike's restaurant.

I remember having a bowl of hot Tapioca cereal with "Ed Jenkins" a classmate from school. I hated the taste. It was like eating fish eggs. Ed loved Tapioca cereal. I just sat and watched him sop up every last drop.

Elizabeth Pharmacy

6

Old And New

We overlook the marvels of Hazelwood's strength in its current housing assets. The majority of the housing throughout Hazelwood predates WWII. Many turn-of-the-century dwellings add a flavor to its historic properties. From the 1930s and 1940s, single-family homes and row houses were intertwined within the conception of the town. Many houses contain lovely sidewalks or stairs leading up to their porches. This follows the style of geographically designed homes which creates an indoor-outdoor, public-private space for the residents.

Porches promote socializing between both residents within the home as well as with neighbors. Early developers built up neighborhood blocks using basic structures that were then individualized to the tastes of buyers. Later with time, residents made changes adding to the unique quality of each home. Many of the row home exist from Tecumseh Street, Chaplin Way and Glenwood Avenue. From Winston Street to Winterburn Avenue there are an abundance of beautiful single living homes across Hazelwood. "A proud close-knit community, bound together by strong relationships and common interests."

"Below the tracks" a term that most locals know. Also known as "Scotch Bottom." The first track of railroad built by Benjamin Franklin Jones Sr. separated Hazelwood into two sections, creating the local term "below the tracks." The railroad was built inland to respect the residents' concern of maintaining the river's charming nature. In 1869 Hazelwood was incorporated into the city, and by the following year the railway had spurred iron and steel industries, railroading, boatbuilding and the river trade.

Immigrants from Scotland were the first settlers in the area of the "Six mile run to the Point of Pittsburgh." Thus called "Scotch Bottom." When the Scottish moved out of Scotch Bottom, the Slavs and Hungarians moved in, and even today there is a large Slavic community around the "Three Mile Run" to Greenfield.
St. Ann's Roman Catholic Church was built in 1924 for an estimated price of $100,000 and for many years provided Hungarian families a Hungarian language school for their youngsters.

Below the tracks was a place I could ride my bike throughout the neighborhood and know I'll be safe. Level streets created a bicycle paradise for the young. My cousins lived on Langhorn Street, in the backpart of the community. From Langhorn Street, I would ride my bicycle to Courtland Street, make a left turn onto Lytle Street, another left ontoTecumseh Street, finally back on Langhorn Street. Many of the homeswere "row houses" at typical urban city living.

Crossing over the railroad tracks on the Elizabeth Street Bridge was a unique sight. There was a bowling alley that sat at the right end base of the bridge. 35 West Elizabeth Street rested Saint Ann's bowling alley. This bowling alley was not just a bowling alley. It was a "Duckpin" bowling alley. Duckpin balls are 4 3⁄4 inches to 5 inches in diameter, weighing about 3 lb. 6 oz to 3 lb. 12 oz each and lack finger holes. They are thus significantly smaller than those used in ten-pin bowling games. The game was fun to play, but hard to get strikes. Saint Anne's bowling alley also had bingo and Bauchi courts on the lower level.

Elisabeth Bridge

Glen-Hazel is a neighborhood in Pittsburgh, Pennsylvania's east of Hazelwood. Situated along the Monongahela River, most of Glen-Hazel is bordered by Hazelwood and shares a small section with Squirrel Hill South to the northeast. The Glenwood Bridge across the Monongahela connects Glen-Hazel to another Pittsburgh neighborhood, Hays, to the south. With the influx of people moving into Hazelwood in 1942, parts of Glen Hazel became a federal government housing project for the defense industry workers. The Housing Authority through the city of Pittsburgh managed the site for the government, and in 1952 purchased the project converting it to low-income housing. The wartime project was gradually replaced by new housing. In 1975 the Housing Authority opened a new 153-unit high-rise for the elderly and this was followed by a 104-unit townhouse development in 1976.

Glen-Hazel over lays Hazelwood Greenway-Elizabeth to Kinglake. The Greenway covers a 1.2 mile delightful out and back trail which features a great wooded setting and is good for all skill levels. The Hazelwood Greenway is one of the original greenways in Pittsburgh. It is less active than seldom seen, and maintenance of the greenway is focused more on conservation. The trail is primarily used for hiking, walking, nature trips, and bird watching and is accessible year-round. "A maintained hiking path in the middle of Hazelwood connecting to our lands to enjoy." Many take their children to get out of the house for a pleasant adventure.

Churches were active in the Hazelwood area. Johnston Avenue Baptist Church, First Hungarian Reformed Church, St. Paul's Lutheran Church, Morningstar Baptist Church. The Church of the Good Shepherd (Episcopal) was established in Glenwood in 1868 with many prominent Pittsburghers as members of the congregation, such as the Burgwins, Pauls, Macrums, Coxes, and Cowens. St. Ann's Roman Catholic Church, Hazelwood Christian Church and St. Stephen's Roman Catholic Church, whose first building in 1870 was located at the Grove Station. Because of the great influx of Catholics, Irish and Italian, into the area, the present structure at the corner of Second Avenue and Elizabeth Street was built.

.

The civic and fraternal lodges of Hazelwood have played a key role in the development of the community. These groups are the Independent Order of Odd Fellows, Lodge No. 1043; Knights of Pythias, Hazelwood Lodge No. 130; Joppa Lodge, F & AM; Hazelwood Moose Lodge No. 486; American-Hungarian Association; Kiwanis Club of Hazelwood-Greenfield; Martin-O'Donnell Post 274, VFW; Hibernian Building and Loan Association; and Fort Black Post 538, American Legion. Many of these groups promoted foodbanks, parades and a diverse social interaction goal for the community. Programs offered educational experiences related to the history or the environment of area. People want to learn, and when they come together to share their experience of knowledge, they celebrate diverse cultures and histories.

Many of the first schools established in Hazelwood are closed today. I will name a few of history's great yesteryear.

Hazelwood School was located at 5000 Second Avenue in the Hazelwood section of Pittsburgh. The school was built in 1872 shortly after the area was annexed to the City of Pittsburgh as the old 23 Ward and was closed on July 1, 1938. The property was sold in 1946 to an American Legion Post for $7,500.

Gladstone School, located on the corner of Hazelwood Avenue and Gladstone Street, was dedicated on May 7, 1915.
The school replaced the nearby Hazelwood Elementary School. In 1923 an addition to the structure was completed that included several new classrooms and an auditorium that could accommodate approximately four hundred students. In 1926 a new building was built to connect the original structure. The new building contained fourteen classrooms, two playrooms, a swimming pool, and two gymnasiums. Gladstone School was the only building in the entire Pittsburgh public school system that began as an elementary school, changed to a junior high school in 1923, served as a senior high school in 1958, and became a middle school in 1976. After months of testimony from the school board, they voted to keep Gladstone open with a limited enrollment until the buildings were renovated. In June 1998, the school board once again approved closing Gladstone by June 2000 because of the expensive renovations.

Burgwin Elementary School, located at Glenwood Avenue in Hazelwood and borders Glen hazel section of Pittsburgh, was named after the Burgwin family and for the first Principle. The school opened in 1939. The school offered special programs such as the Parent and Child Guidance Program, the Life Skills program , the Women's Center and Shelter Program. The building is 3 stories in height. It accommodates 920 pupils in 22 classrooms and a kindergarten. The school was closed since 2006. Burgwin School is one of 3 schools in the Hazelwood neighborhood in Pittsburgh, Pa., which has closed. In 2006, Pittsburgh closed 23 of its 66 schools and has since closed or proposed closure for four others. Burgwin Elementary is now operated as a charter school, called "Propel Hazelwood." Propel Hazelwood supports passion and encourages dreams. Their mission is to inspire achievement through critical thinking, evidence-based understanding and innovation.

On September 15, 1902, Reverend Daniel Devlin, pastor for St. Stephen's church, purchased property from the family of the late Simon Johnson. The property was located at the corner of East Elizabeth Street and Gertrude Street. A convent was built for the Sisters of Charity, and in 1910, a new school was erected. Saint Stephen's school was directed by the Sisters. In the early years, few people had cars, so kids walked to School. Buses were unheard of.
In them years, lunchrooms or cafeterias were non-existent. If you brought your lunch to school, you ate it in one of the classrooms.
I attended St. Stephen's from 1966 to 1973. I experienced great and exciting memories while going to St. Stephen's. There were a variety of Sisters at St. Stephen's school from smiley faces to as mean as mean could get, especially towards the boys. A quote from Cathy DiThomas Farkal. "I loved the St. Stephen's bazaar, and I loved Trick or Treating atthe Convent. The nuns were so nice. When the convent was being demolished all the nuns were crying."

The day I stole a kiss will always be a great memory for me. I'm sure she has forgotten. But not me.

I STOLE A KISS

When I was ten,

I stole a kiss from a girl in English class.

Watching this girl, my silent thoughts would not pass.

Diane sat in her polka-dot dress.

Her curly brown hair had a tint of hazel tress.

She seemed too pretty for a young man's heart.

The time must be right, or my dreams will part.

The class was silent,

only the chosen will speak.

The teacher stands erect with her pointer so sleek.

I may be a thief who loves to take a chance.

I hope Sister Ann will not give me a glance.

Quietly I crawled out of my seat.

And before she knew,

a kiss was placed upon her cheek.

In my seven plus years at St. Stephens school. I have been kicked in the ass, hit with rulers, cheeks pinched and sent to the corner of the room. But I never talked back to one teacher or nun. I respected them to the highest standards.

Once among the largest grade schools in the diocese of Pittsburgh Pa., with an enrollment of 1,400 students during the 1960s and 1970s, St. Stephen had only 56 pupils projected for the 2005-06 school year. 112 years after it opened its doors, the school closed in June of 2005. The building is now the Spartan Community Center of Hazelwood. A group of alumni formed a Non-Profit Organization in September 2016 supporting the Greater Hazelwood Community. Currently it is the home of Fishes and Loaves, Meals on Wheels, Three rivers Village School, Center of Life Educational Programs, Art Excursions, Unity through Creativity, Pittsburgh Players Theatre Group and more. The building is still alive.

St. Stephen's church

Built 1902

St. Anne's church

Built 1924

Episcopal Church of the Good Shepherd

C. 1933

Christian Church

Fountain of Life

Former Hazelwood Presbyterian Church

Built 1921

First Hungarian Lutheran Church

First Hungarian Reformed Church

Built 1904

St. Paul Lutheran Church

Now Holy Cross Chapel

St. John The Evangelist Baptist Church

First Church built in 1920/caught fire in 1942/Rebuilt here in 1958

St. John Chrysostom Byzantine Catholic Church. Built 1935

Famed pop artist, Andy Warhol and his family were members of St. John

Morning Star Missionary

Baptist Church

C. 1892

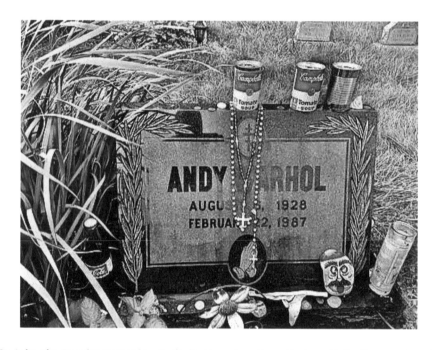

St. John the Baptist Byzantine Catholic Cemetery is an Eastern Catholic cemetery in Bethel Park Pennsylvania.
He is buried alongside his parents, Julia and Andrej Warhol.

Andy Warhol prompt: THEY ALWAYS SAY TIME CHANGES EVE-RYTHING, BUT YOU ACTUALLY HAVE TO CHANGE THEM YOURSELF.

Hunting twenty-five feet off the ground, a young bird whispers to my ear.
A soft unforgettable sound streamed with a magical tone.

Perched gently on my shoulder,
full of life waiting for dawn.
Did this happen before?
The young bird speaks of birth underlying our world.

Metaphors mention the earth with no effect, only the blind living in present..
Humanity is the soul for living.

Nature cries in silence unseen.
I used to be respectable as your Gods.
Now steel and concrete scourge this planet.

Tree of life is scrap wood turned to ash.
The human has stolen more from me, the core of living.

As I look at this young bird I sob because of progress.
I sob because of greed.
I sob because we are losing a gift.

With in minutes the little bird flies away.
I climbed down my tree.
Aye. My tree.
Nature's beauty.
I drive in my car back to the steel and concrete.

Built around 1900...

**Former Free Methodist Episcopal Church, now home to Praise Temple Deliverance -
corner of Glenwood Ave. and Almeda St.**

Religious belief can improve the function of democracy.
Religion offers humility. Believing makes us humble in God's presence.
In truth, God is all perfect and we are not. Faith is a learning process
through our entire life. Studying religion helps us learn the complexities
of diverse cultures and to improve our inner self with peace.
Our life is affected by religious convictions and opinions. By being able
to understand the basic concepts in different religions, we will develop
into a better society.

Hazelwood School was located at 5000 Second Avenue in the Hazelwood.
Built in 1872. Closed on July 1, 1938

Saint Stephen's School Erected 1910

Currently Spartan Community Center of Hazelwood

Gladstone School 1915.

Addition Built 1926

Burgwin Elementary 1939

Is now a charter school, called "Propel Hazelwood."

Nestled between Abriola Autato-Parts and the Elizabeth Pharmacy sits the Italian Village Pizza. It's an outpost of a local pizzeria chain with a menu of pizzas, hoagies, catzones and other Italian staples. Their pizza has great flavors and fresh ingredients. Definitely a must when it comes to a fantastic pizza. Directly across Italian Village Pizza is Automotive Medic. Automotive Medic is a locally owned complete auto repair shop with friendly and fair service.

The last bakery that I remember on Second Ave. was Retenaur's Bakery. Retenaur's was booming during the J&L Steel mill days. After major shutdowns with the steel industry, the bakery closed. However, my cousin Maggie Reider shared her latest endeavor to me. The La Gourmandine French bakery opened in Hazelwood. Fabien and Lisanne Moreau born and raised in France are the founders of the La Gourmandine bakery. Both their parents grew up in the French countryside except for Lisanne's mom who is from Pittsburgh. Lisanne would visit often to the Steel City to visit her Grandparents, family and friends. Eventually she moves to Pittsburgh. Fabien agreed to follow in hopes to open his own business. Fabien went to school at the Lenôtre Culinary Institute in Paris where he learned the artistry in culinary science. In June of 2010, La Gourmandine bakery and pastry shop opened in Lawrenceville. Four years later, in 2014, Lisanne and Fabien opened their second shop in Mt. Lebanon. March 20, 2017, La Gourmandine bakery opened in Hazelwood. This became one of my favorite places when visiting Hazelwood.

Next to La Gourmandine is the Hazelwood Market at 5009 Second Avenue. Best place for Faygo and all types of snacks. The owner is very friendly and welcoming.

La Gourmandine Bakery

Dianne Shenk
Dylamato's Market
Your Neighborhood Grocery

I used to drive through Hazelwood on my way to work at the Allegheny County Airport (2007-2009), where I worked for 3 years. On my way through town, I noticed Dimperio's grocery store and often thought about stopping but never did. Then I saw the articles in the Post Gazette when it closed. The next year (2010) I enrolled in a master's in food studies program at Chatham University and our first semester I learned about food deserts. The next semester (Jan 2011) I was in a class where we had to do a project around food, and I decided to come to Hazelwood and get out of my car and explore what food was available in the community - Hazelwood is a designated food desert community. First stops were the Rite Aid and SR Market, then on to Elizabeth Pharmacy, where I ran into Ursula Craig. I told her I was looking at food in the community and she sent me around the corner to HI (Hazelwood Initiative) and Jim Richter. Jim listened to me and sent me on to the group that was exploring a buying club in Hazelwood with the help of Lisa Stolarski. I sat in on all the meetings that spring to write the bylaws and get the organization started and volunteered during the first distributions. I was assigned to Hazelwood Towers to do outreach and got to know the manager, Bill Kulina. Well, I've been working with the Fishes and Loaves Buying Club as a customer, volunteer, steering committee member, advisor and now a Board Member since spring of 2011. This role gave me legitimacy in the community, and I got to know residents of Hazelwood Towers and Roselle Court (two low-income high rise Through all of this time, my focus has been on both getting my own small business started and also creating a business model that is collaborative with other small businesses in the community. My store works at sourcing food from other small businesses - I purchase pastries from MeeMee's Tis So Sweet Bakery and have collaborated to help get the St Stephens Hall (now Spartan Center) commercial kitchen online and available for vendors like Elite Treats and Specialty Feasts, Mee Mee's Tis So Sweet Bakery and Dylamato's Market (we rented the kitchen for 3-4 hours once a week for preparation of our salads and sandwich fillings for 3 years).

In 2019 we renovated our own kitchen with 2 ovens and moved our production there as well as opening the space for Mee Mee's Tis So Sweet Bakery, who now does all her production on site at Dylamato's Market. I have also purchased fresh produce from a number of backyard gardeners and urban farmers who are actively growing in Hazelwood. In 2018, I hired Hazelwood resident interior designers – Rooke Creative – to renovate the front section of the store as a space where community makers could display their creations in a consignment space. We have room for a tee-shirt designer, several ceramic artists, 3 candle makers, as well as jewelry, knitting creations and hand-made incense. This space is an opportunity for community members to begin growing a business or finding a way to gain a little extra income from a homegrown hobby.

When the pandemic hit in March of 2020, we stayed open as an essential business. We saw our business grow quickly as people needed a place to shop and we offered home deliveries and drive-by pickups for those who didn't want to come into the store. Over that summer, our business grew until we were operating at 50% higher sales than before the pandemic started. This has slowed down a little over the winter, but we continue to have sales high enough to sustain our current employees and keep the business financially viable.

Dylamato's

The Carnegie Library of Pittsburgh Hazelwood Branch, located at 4748 Monongahela Street was built in 1899. It was added to the city of Pittsburgh Historic designations on July 28, 2004. Before it's closure, the 103-year-old library featured a mahogany circulation desk with a distinctive stained-glass dome in the ceiling. The library was one of the town's main social and cultural centers with a storytelling area for children and a basement auditorium where local theatrical groups staged plays and musicals. It was a highly active library with a variety of programs going on during the week. Efforts are underway to preserve and reuse the former Carnegie Library building in Hazelwood. When the library first opened, transportation was quite different from bus routes today. Only a few people had their own horse and buggy. Many walked to the complex to enjoy reading. The building cost $40,000 with 5000 books in the opening collection. The wall decorations had framed photographs and plaster casts of folks and scenes not only from Pittsburgh but other parts of the world. As for me, I was not much of a bookworm. I enjoyed the many programs and shows that the library offered.

The library reopened its third location in a renovated church on Second Avenue in June 2014. $2.4 million was the cost to restore the building that doubled its original 3,500-square-foot space to 7,000 square feet. As part of the Hazelwood Center, the library also brought together programs from the Trying Together and the local Head Start to the Family Support Center. The library features a children's room decorated with a large metal art piece by Homestead artist David Lewis: and there is an entire wall painted with animals amid the trees of the "Hazel Woods."

Hazelwood Library

Hazelwood Library

7

Glen-Hazel "The Projects"

Growing up in Hazelwood, I never knew the true meaning behind the Projects. My grandmother and I would visit some friends in Glen-Hazel, but I could not understand why the homes looked like army barracks. I decided to share what I have found.

During World War II, urban areas across the United States faced housing shortages that threatened the industrial production vital to the serve the war. Due to the massive steel manufacturing, Pittsburgh attracted large numbers of people seeking employment. This heavy employment caused many workers looking to settle into the region or community. Given that the iron and steel industries, railroading and boating, they became part of a large-scale workforce for Hazelwood, Homestead and Duquesne.

As a result, the federal government built a housing project in the Glen-Hazel Heights for the defense industry workers. Rents ranged from $25 per month for three rooms and a bath to $32.50 a month for six rooms and a bath. The Housing Authority of Pittsburgh managed the site for the government, and in 1952 purchased the project converting it to low-income housing plan. With time, the buildings started falling apart because of poor construction. In 1975 a new 153-unit high rise for the elderly was opened, followed by a 104-unit townhouse development in 1976. Today Glen-Hazel supports the Kane Community Center and a Behavioral Health Center through Mercy Hospital.

Above 1940's, 1960's and 1980's

Glen-Hazel "The Projects"

Today 2021

Glen-Hazel

While driving down Hazelwood Avenue, I made a right turn onto Sylvan Avenue. Along the street, I noticed a group of people working in the wooded area parallel to the road. I stopped to ask what they were doing. The group was working for Grow Pittsburgh. Grow Pittsburgh is a nonprofit organization that serves the community to educate the needs and priorities for growing food in local neighborhoods. Early March is the time to clean up the area and lay compost for gardening. Because the area is widely shaded, they will plant mushrooms, lettuce and maybe some beets. Grow Pittsburgh holds regular garden work shops throughout the growing season, and access to their Info Hub for the latest urban techniques. Western Pennsylvania Conservancy is a partner with Grow Pittsburgh to provide material and support.

Greg, Stacy and Laura

March 2021

8

Games People Play

     Growing up there was always something to do. I was never in the house. You could say "early out and last one in." We played in alleys, we played on streets, sidewalks, backyards, basketball courts, baseball fields, football fields and we made our own field in the middle of the woods. Anywhere possible we were there.

The Oil Field
It wasn't just life; this was our world.
Rise and shine.
Breakfast at seven in the morning.
"Cold cereal and then a dash out the door"

Four of my friends and I would run to the local baseball field and play America's past time.
"Baseball'
Nicky, Matt; Luke and Bobby were the players.
Nicky was my best friend. We were like a tag team.
Matt and Luke were brothers.
They would always get on each other, especially if one made an error in the game.
Bobby was a little older.
He was a wise ass, a jackass and a pain in the ass.
A bully of his own.
Everything was his way.
"You know the kind"

Racing up Nansen Street, felt like running to the top of mountain, only with potholes.
Trees protruded from each side of the road consumed light making shadows come to life.

Reaching the top, we made a sharp right onto Hazelwood Avenue.
Hazelwood Avenue was constructed with "Belgium cut" stone blocks.
In the rain, the blocks were slippery as ice.
You would never ride a bike.
It would be wipeout city.
And the cars would creep five miles per hour down the hill.
Otherwise, they would end up in someone's living room.

About a quarter of a mile walk and we were standing at the backstop.
Now this baseball field was unique.
The locals called the field, the "Oil Field."
The proper name was the "Gladstone" field. Which was the high school and grade school located about a quarter of a mile down Hazelwood Ave.

This field was sprayed monthly with oil.
Yes oil!
This prevented dust, mud, grass and bugs.
"Who would believe this today"?

The Oil Field was hard and fast. Slick when wet.
You could smell the field a block away.
You definitely didn't want to slide.
But at all costs,
to win the game we did everything
and anything.
Slide, jump and roll.
Covered with a black type of tar,
our clothes would be stained as our bodies would be in pain.
We were never allowed in the house with our shoes on.
That's when you would get a tongue lashing.

Now how the heck do you play a baseball game with only five players?
The best way is.
One player between shortstop and third base,
the second player at left center outfield,
last the pitcher, first baseman and a catcher.
With a lefty batter, we would switch the outfield player to right-center
and short to second.

If a right-hand batter hits the ball to between second base and first base
he's automatically out.
With a left-hand batter, it will be the opposite. Hit between second and
third you were out. We played at the far end of the field. The cliffs were
at left field. If you hit the cliffs, it was a homerun.

Morning until dusk,
we played baseball all summer.
The girls would watch,
never allowed on the field.
Fear of staining their clothes and white tennis shoes.

There may be a few fights about certain plays on the field.
We would be rolling around and look like we're ready to be
feathered.Funny no one got hurt.

"Man, here comes the older kids"
"Them damn bullies"
They would kick us off the field so they could play.

One day they got out of hand.
Picking on us kids so freaking bad,
they started throwing equipment all over the field.
Gloves, bats and baseballs launched all over the place.

One kid, his name was Mick.
He looked like a sumo wrestler.
"A big fat dough boy"
Mick threw us around like rag dolls.
Swearing and calling us names.

We ran
and ran,
Empty handed and all.
Our equipment was left at the field.

When we reached home,
Nicky told his brother "Johnny" what happened at the Oil field.
Johnny hopped on his minibike and sped up Nansen Street.

By the time we reach the field.

Johnny was powerlifting Mick over his head.
Johnny threw Mick on the hill side.
A hundred yards away, we heard a thud.
That was the last time these kids picked on us.

In the evening we would watch men play softball on the Oil Field.
These players crushed the ball.
If they hit a ball in the outfield, you would lose sight of it.
Within seconds, the catch was made.
This was amazing.
Each player had grace, speed and power.

In the late summer, Gladstone would be practicing football on the oil
field. They were big and fast. The thrill of the chase is the ultimate high.
Spectators would be sitting on the sidewalk cheering the players.
A young kid would love to be like them.

The Courts

Basketball was the worst sport for me to play. You could call me the one-armed dribbler. I was the short straw in a pickup game.
The majority of the games I played were at Gladstone school. The court in front of the school was always busy. Streetball tournaments were organized on weekends. Popular street basketball was 21, Roughhouse, 33 and Crunch. 21 is played with 3 to 5 players on a half court. As for me, I was lousy. My daughter could whip my butt.

The Alley

Large overhanging branches extended like hands ready to carry you away.
This tree can grow a majestic one hundred and fifty feet high into the sky.
The circumference can reach eight feet. It would take four to five kids holding hands to rap around this tree.
Green fruit would fall from the branches. The fruit was as large as a baseball. You would never see anyone park a car under the tree, otherwise there would be dents covering the hood, roof and trunk.
This tree known as a walnut tree was massive.

You could not eat the fruit right away.
Inside was like tar or black grease covering a nut. People would gather peel and let sit for a time. Then crack and eat.

Alongside this walnut tree concealed an alley with no name.
This alley granted imagination and creativity, a dead-end utopia for all children in the neighborhood.
Every game you can think of was played on this street.

Bicycle jumping off wooden platforms introduced new thrills for the young at hearted.
Sometimes we would compete to see how airborne the bicyclists could go.
Every once in a while, there would be a wipe out.

No problem, get up and try it again.
The trick was to spring up at the end of wooden jump, this would give
you distance.

Baseball and football was always exciting.
During our baseball games each player had to bat from the opposite side.
This made it difficult for the hitter.
The baseball usually traveled a short distance. How ever the switch
hitters killed the ball.

Tag football games were played on asphalt roads. Tackle would be
disastrous. There were too many injuries. Sometimes there would be a
few accidental takedowns. The end result bloody knees, elbows and a
bump on the noggin.
Big boys crying all the way home.

Street hockey was pure unadulterated hockey.
All you needed was a ball, hockey stick and a goal.
Fast exhilarating competition drove a kid to win.
After a certain amount of time, we alternated offensive and defense.

Of course, checking was limited,
you would either end up against a brick wall or down into the woods.

There were more games like kickball to wrestling.
We would be muddy beyond recognition.
Badminton, Frisbee and nights of hide and seek throughout the
neighborhood.

At the corner entrance to the alley sat a small one level house.
It was light blue in color, box shaped with a flat slanted roof.
The siding was similar to shingles on a roof, a gritty type texture
overlapping each other.
There was an older couple that lived in the home.
Volio was their last name'
D'Angelo and Mabel two little Italians.
Babushka and all that floral color design.

While playing in the alley, you would see the curtains open slowly
and then close.
The curtains would open about two inches.
It was creepy, like a black cat
waiting for a mouse to devour.

This mysterious manner
didn't faze us kids
until one ghastly day.

One kid hit a baseball that traveled up to Volio's house.
All of a sudden, a little lady dashed out the side-door, snatched the ball
and scurried back in the house. She was fast like lightning striking a
tree. Everyone was dumbfounded upon seeing this little woman steal the
ball.

What is next?
We will go knock on the door and ask.
The Volio's would not answer the door.
The widow curtains on the right side of the door opened slowly then
closed.
Not a word was said.
We just ran away.

This was the beginning to the end of great games, but there was a day for
revenge. Not! Some bad boy grabbed a dead bird and placed it in their
mailbox.
Of course, a neighbor spotted the kid in the act and screamed at him to
getit out.

Organized Baseball and Football

Baseball was the first organized sport I played. It was with the Hazelwood Little League Association. The field was named after Joe Pardi and located on Johnston Ave. above the Burgwin pool. In the beginning I was a bench warmer. Every game I would warm up the pitchers and eventually I won the starting position as a catcher. There was one game I remember very well. A player was barreling down to home plate and the throw from left field was right on target into my Glove. Applying the tag, I got mowed down like a blade of grass. Knocked out cold, but I held the ball and he was out.

Who was Joseph (Joe) Pardi? Well, I found some information I would like to share. It was in the Pittsburgh Catholic, April 14, 1960.

"Joseph Pardi, longtime district basketball and football official and coach of St. Stephen's grade football team, died unexpectedly last Tuesday in his sleep at his home, 88 Flower Ave., Hazelwood. Pardi coached football at St. Stephen's for the past 15 years and Dorothy Garrlty Is timekeeper. St. Mary of Sharpsburg, coached by Virginia Aufman, won the Section B title and Sacred Heart of East End, coached by Carol Truschel, copped Section C. and was a member of the West Penn Basketball Officials Association.

He was also active in Little League baseball and was well known in Hazelwood for his youth work. Pardi was buried from St. Stephen Church last Saturday."

Another favorite for the baseball players was the Hazelwood Memorial Day Parade. We felt like professional baseball players. The high school bands marched in front of us. People cheering on both sides of Second Avenue. After the parade, I would run to the 5 and 10 store. A couple Pittsburgh Pirates would be sitting behind a table and giving out autographs. I got Richie Hebner, Dave Cash, Al Oliver. Hebner was known for working as a gravedigger at a cemetery run by his father during the offseason. He was also a good ice hockey player. I would see him at South Park's Ice-skating rink in the early sessions.

Most of my organized football was with St Stephen's grade school. We practiced and played our games at Burgwin field. At ten, eleven and twelve years of age, we were like the dirty dozen.
We had our little secrets in the huddle, not even the coach would know. I think because our practices were worse than the games. The first time I got head slapped I did not know what the "F" was going on. The coach would throw out the ball in the field. Two players raced to the ball. The first player that got the ball, had to hold it while the other player "kicked" your ass to get it. Diving, spearing, whatever he could do. And of course, I would have to go against my best friend Nicky. I got the ball first all the time, but after about 10 minutes I was whipped. I could not hold the ball anymore. That's all she wrote.
Nicky had a strong powerful grip. I could never get the ball back. During our games. we would gang tackle like in the movie "The Longest Yard." When piling up on the offense player, the referees could never see what was happening at the bottom. Yea, us boys were saints, "Not."

Swimming

Growing up in Hazelwood, most water sports were under a hose or fire hydrant. Running through a sprinkler was a blast. Imagination was the perfect ingredient for backyard fun. When it is summer and the temperatures rise, kids love to cool down in water. Fun with sprinklers can be more than just running through and screaming. Cartwheels, front and back crab walks, or scissor jump through the sprinkler are always some favorites. Infront of a fire hydrant you had to be careful not to get blown away. Most of the older kids could withstand the power of the spray.
As for public swimming pools, my mother would take me to the Burgwin pool or Mineral Beach in Finleyville Pa. If not playing baseball on the weekends, we went to Mineral Beach most of the time. Mineral Beach was a unique pool. The pool consisted of two sections. The first section was the shallow end that had a gradual slope. Many pool chairs were lined across the edge for parents to dip their feet into the water while watching kids splash around. The adult area had two diving boards. One low and the other high.

In the 1950's, 1960's and 1970's, kids were expected to go outside and play. Such play was not often a sport. We played with imagination and ingenuity. Sometimes our creativity would get us in trouble.

Hide and Go Seek. Kick the Can, (Hong Kong). Hopscotch. Mother May I. Tree Climbing. Tree Shacks. Ground Shacks. Jump Rope. We entertained ourselves for hours.

Hong Kong is a game similar to Kick the Can or Hide and Seek. The game portrays hunter and prey. Someone hides and the other person comes looking for them. A can is placed on the ground. The person "it," covers their eyes and counts to a set number before going on the hunt. The prey has a choice to hide or run to the can and throw it before the hunter gets back to home base. That will free the people they have captured. Starting all over again.

Another game that most city kids know is called the Hub Cap Game. Now what the heck is this? Well, the game is played by hiding in the woods next to a street. First, we gather old hub caps before we start. Then the fun begins. When a car drives by, we would throw a hub cap out on the road and watch the driver stop. He would look at all four wheels and realize it wasn't his hub cab that fell off. What a silly game, but it was fun.

Many of these activities kept us healthy. We developed strength, speed and coordination. Today I see very few pick-up games on courts, Ballfields or in neighborhoods.

9

Steps of Hazelwood

The landscape in Hazelwood can be very appealing or a brutal enemy. The hilly terrain provides rewarding adventures throughout the neighborhood. Pittsburgh has a collection of nearly 800 sets of city owned steps connecting communities and providing access to many public amenities. This linkage is a critical asset for Hazelwood's pedestrian network. In the same sharp way, reaching the top summit, the view can be a breathtaking beauty. Maintaining these individual steps and boardwalks—is an enormous challenge for the city. Repairing or replacing a staircase structure is comparable to undertaking a small bridge project. As a result, the city prioritizes each project to make the most impact for the people walking in the hilliest neighborhoods. Pittsburgh is known for the city having the most steps in America, and second in the world to Venice. Living on Nansen Street was a great step climbing experience. Running up to the top of Nansen was a challenging thrill. There are two different observations when walking or running from point A to point B. Looking from the bottom-up, damn! Looking from the top-down, wow! A wonderful experience in my youth. Today, I had the same reaction when I drive up and down Nansen. Unbelievable! I am extremely fortunate and proud to share this with my family and friends.

Eddington Street Steps Lower Kilbourne Street

Pittsburgh Community Walk No. 48

Nansen Street Pittsburgh Community Walk No. 23

Tullymet Street Pittsburgh Community Walk No. 30

Gladstone Street and Parnell Street

Dido Street

Dido Street Est: 1920

Doing some research on local streets. I had a response from a lady about **Dido Street**. Jeanette Davis offered some great information from a photograph she had of her great-grandfather Sylvester Larkin (age mid to late 20's). In the previous picture, Sylvester Larkin (1899-1988) is seen fishing down the ravine off Kilbourne, formerly Flowers Ave. He had his home built on the corner of Tesla and Kilbourne in the 1920's . As to this day-March 30, 2018, the home remains ownership in her family.

10

Panther Hollow Lake

Panther Hollow Lake is a man-made lake located in Schenley Park. Schenley Park is located in Pittsburgh, Pennsylvania, between the neighborhoods of Oakland, Greenfield, and Squirrel Hill. It is also listed on the National Register of Historic Places as a historic district. The lake was constructed from an already existing but a smaller body of water at the site between the years of 1907 and 1909. Panther Hollow Lake was once a great recreational area that included a boat house alongside the lake. Families would rent boats and picnic throughout the day. Structured above the lake sits Panther Hollow Bridge. What makes the bridge incredibly unique is the layout of four bronze sculpted panthers positioned at each corner. These panthers symbolize guardians on entering and exiting the valley, and the hollow is named for the mountain lions once native to the area.

During my time growing up in Hazelwood, Panther Hollow Lake was a great escape. It didn't matter what I caught. Bluegill, carp, catfish and bass were regularly stocked by the city. My favorite bait store was in my grandmother's kitchen. Canned corn and bread were the easiest to acquire. As for worms, they were harder to get. We would collect them under rocks or dead logs. Corn on a hook with a bobber or sinker and I was set for the day. The lake provided great beauty to the park along with lasting memories to share with your family and friends. Today the lake is in dire need of restoration. The water level is at best five feet deep with the remainder filled with runoff sediment. Panther Hollow trail is a 1.9-mile loop primarily used for hiking, walking, running and wildlife watching.

Panther Hollow Lake

1900'S

1960'S

2021

During the Great Depression, the parks Director Ralph Griswald was successful in establishing FDR's Works Progress Administration projects to enhance the overall City Park grounds, including Schenley Park. The WPA workers built stone bridges (which still bear the chiseled "WPA 1939" brand), created and/or improved roads and trails, cleared the deadwood and streambeds, planted new trees, and even renovated the lake boathouse. They built the stone step system that accesses the lake.

My walking route to Panther Hollow was pretty simple, Nansen Street to Hazelwood Avenue. I would then travel down Hazelwood Avenue until I reached Second Avenue (Irvine Street). Next, I would make a right onto Second Avenue and continue as if I were going to Town. Once I reached the intersection of Greenfield Avenue, I would hop onto the railroad tracks and walk to the back part of Panther Hollow Lake. The trek was a little over 3 miles and would take about an hour to get to the lake. If I rode my bicycle to Panther Hollow, the route was up Hazelwood Avenue by the Calvary Cemetery and make a sharp left on Bigelow Street, right on McCaslin Street, and finally Greenfield Avenue to Panther Hollow Road. Sometimes I would ride to the Pittsburgh Avery, the Phipps Conservatory, the Carnegie Museum and around Forbes Field where the Pirates played.

Phipps Conservatory

11

The Pink House

One of the most unique homes I lived in was on Electric Street. Electric Street is located at the top of East Elizabeth Street and is a dead-end street that may lead to heaven or hell, it all depends on your own view. Now why was this house a one of a kind? The exterior of this house was painted pink and resembled a children's fairy tale.

In the fall of 1970, my mother rented the bottom floor. The bottom was made into an apartment. This was the first time I had a bedroom. A small room with a bed and dresser. I thought I was the luckiest kid in town. Another quality this house had was it bordered woods. Today the area is called the Hazelwood Greenway. The wooded area extends from Electric Street to the Calvary Cemetery and from Kilbourne Street to Johnston Avenue in Glen Hazel. The first couple of weeks living in this apartment-house was very creepy. Many unusual sounds were heard inside and outside our new home. As for being inside, there were small creatures crawling about, sometimes on your skin. "Bugs in the house." Crickey crickets sounding their mating calls were awfully hard to locate, especially when turning the lights on they cease and desist. Centipedes and millipedes love damp places. Seeing one in a sink can drive you nuts. Turn on the hot water and watch them slip and slide down the drain. Cockroaches are very resourceful insects that can live, eat, and breed in your house without you even knowing it. They are great at hide and seek games. Under, over and behind refrigerators, sinks, and in dark drawers or cabinets. Spiders are the worst. I would wake up in the morning with a spider bite on my arm. The bite was like any insect bite with a little itching or rash on the skin.
I hate spiders in the house. As for outside, windy storms would cause concern. There were large walnut and oak trees surrounding the house. Luckily nothing ever happened. One less worry.

The end of Electric Street reached a wooded area with overhanging branches making the road dark and gloomy. This dead end was a great place for stolen, stripped and torched automobiles or trucks. Occasionally I would see a firetruck racing up the street to extinguish the blaze. The auto was left to rust for a year or so. As a result, there were two cars and one truck crumbling away at the butt end of Electric Street.

The back of Electric St. opened into a kid's oasis. A paradise for climbing trees and nature's wild. This was a great escape from the city's infrastructure. Shades of dark green covered the woodland floor through the speckled sunlight of towering oaks. A small spring flourished with minnows, crawfish, frogs and lizards that followed the hillside into the city. Garter snakes bask during the day, which means they will soak up the sun on top of logs or rocks.

There is a simple method for catching crayfish and lizards. Just stand in a crick and lift stones and wait for the current to flush away the mirky silt. Attack from behind and scoop with your hands. You may want to grab behind the head of a crayfish for not to get pinched by their claws.

As for snakes. I would use a forked stick to trap their head against the ground or log. Wait until the snake calms down and then carefully pinch his head on both sides to pick him up. Now what would I do with these critters? Well, I would take them home and stink up the house. One time I caught 6 snakes and brought them home in a terrarium container. I dropped the container in the cellar and all the snakes escaped. It was a panic episode. I only recovered 4 snakes. I kept quiet. Today I wonder if they ever had little ones.

October 27, 1917

December 23, 2006

Natural Spring April 2021

With all the wild excursions I had in the woods, one unique discovery stands out on its own. I was walking across the hillside behind Electric Street and wandered upon a hole the size of a baseball in the middle of the woods. Thinking it was the home of a snake, I found a five-foot tree limb to thrust into the hole. The limb went completely down the hole, unseen like an abyss of eternal nothing. It was very dark and deep, so I ran home to fetch a flashlight and a shovel to investigate. Looking down the hole was amazing. It opened into a small room about the size of a walk-in closet. I started digging around the hole as fast as a black bear digging for a rodent. Within minutes, the hole was large enough to climb down the cavity.

What lies beneath the hillside is about to be discovered by a ten-year-old boy. This was a coal mine leading deep into the ground for me to explore. All the mines in the Hazelwood area are empty, abandoned and over a hundred years old. Most are covered over from years of time. However, sinkholes appear on streets, under homes and hillsides, causing severe damage to the area.

Climbing down the hole was not too difficult. There were rocks and roots protruding from the sides making it easy to grasp. Once at the bottom, you made a left turn into a small area about four feet high and ten feet across. The ceiling was a flat smooth rock structure with sweating water droplets clinging from the top. Continuing forward, I had to crawl through a small hole that opened into a full-size room that you could stand in. The floor slanted down about forty degrees to another tunnel. On the next level you would crawl through a hole about twenty feet to a dead end. Apparently, the tunnel had collapsed. "Could you imagine the vast maze of coal mines throughout city?" "I can picture a coal miner going deep into the ground with a pickaxe and a caged yellow canary to work all day." After taking a picture of this mine and showing it to my mother, that was the last time I was allowed to go.

Twenty feet underground going into the second room

Hazelwood Greenway Trail—-Runs from East Elizabeth Street to Longview Street. This is a 1.2 mile moderately trafficked out and back trail with great forest settings and is good for all skill levels. The trail is primarily used for hiking, walking, nature trips, and bird watching and is accessible year-round. Dogs are also able to use this trail. This area of Hazelwood used to be a dumping ground for polluters. The city declared it a greenway, protecting it from future development. Volunteers from PA Cleanways and the Student Conservation— Association worked to rid the greenway of 10 tons of household trash, six tons of scrap metal, 100 bags of recyclables, and 72 tires. Working with the International Mountain Biking Association and the Hazelwood Initiative, they eventually developed a broad navigational trail system within the city. Taking care of mother nature will improve the quality of life by maximizing the substantial public health, environmental, and economic benefits for the future to come.

12

Lytle Café

Hazelwood is like a magnet. No matter how far you move away, memories always draw people back to visit their hometown.

Denise Perris (DeDe), proprietor of the Lytle Café for over 48 years, has the honor of being the last bar existing in Hazelwood to date. Denise and her husband John were born and raised in Hazelwood and grew up right down the street from Lytle Café.

In 1973, the married couple purchased the bar from the Bence family and transformed it into one of Hazelwood's favorite taverns to socialize.

Walking into the Lytle Café provides a nostalgic look at the golden age of history and has attracted many interesting people to share their stories and laughs. In the day, it was a popular place for steel mill workers and railroad workers for a warm lunch. Since then, this revered watering hole has cultivated many loyal locals thanks to the numerous events provided for entertainment.

DeDe had an artistic talent for decorating the bar on special occasions and holidays. The Lytle was home to themes like Luaus, Halloween parties, Greek week, Italian week, Mexican week and even Circus week. Everyone dressed for each event. Neighbors would cook their special dishes and bring them to the parties. The Lytle was the talk of the town. "Hot sausage Wednesday" is when the old-timers and regulars get together and share their stories while enjoying a home cooked hot sausage sandwich. Wednesdays at noon, seniors share stories from their youth that may have never been told before. This is an ideal way to connect with generations of historical events and personal stories to pass on. Every person on this Earth has an amazing story to tell, one that belongs to no one else. Memories matter, so why not share your life's experiences.

The regular old timers, John Gergacs, John Kish, Bobby Perris, Floyd Clawson, Fritz Phillips and Harry Bolton continue to this day to gather and eat the famous "Hot Sausage" at the Lytle.

On Memorial Day, the Lytle Café holds a special observance for all the men and women who served in the armed forces. Every year the people of Hazelwood, the mayor and veterans gather in front of the war memorial adornment to honor our military personnel who have died in the performance of their duties while serving in the United States Armed Forces. From its red, white and blue sidewalk to the plaques and flags behind the gate, Dede and John have kept the spirit alive and well.

Despite the fruitful and chaotic times, the Lytle Café has endured life's changes. The walls are decorated with sports heroes and famous movie stars. "Frank Sinatra was John's favorite singer." This bar is a part of Hazelwood history. They thrive to stay alive.

December 24, 2008, John passed away. **Dede and her children Denise Perris Provident (Niecy), Camille Perris Clifford and Michelle Perris Auberzinsky** have continued with great honor and pride to keep the Lytle alive. Every Sunday the bar is closed to the public but opened for the family to gather for dinner and spend precious time together.
The Lytle Café will make you smile.

Lytle Café

13

Calvary Cemetery

In 1886, a 200-acre tract of land was purchased by the Catholic Diocesan of Pittsburgh Pennsylvania. The acreage was converted into a Cemetery located in the Hazelwood area with rolling hills and scenic views. It remains the largest cemetery in the Roman Catholic diocesan of Pittsburgh. The first burial took place in June 1888.

The cemetery includes two exquisite chapel mausoleums, a garden crypt establishment, a mausoleum set aside for the bishops of Pittsburgh and many other developments. There are also numerous distinguished people buried at the cemetery.

Frank John Gorshin Jr. (April 5, 1933 – May 17, 2005) a character actor, impressionist, and comedian. He was perhaps best known as an impressionist. His most famous acting role was as the Riddler on the television series Batman, a performance for which he was nominated for an Emmy Award and catapulted the character to become a major villain for the superhero.

Richard S. Caliguiri (October 20, 1931 – May 6, 1988) who served as the mayor of Pittsburgh, Pennsylvania from 1977 until his death in 1988.

Vincent Martin Leonard (December 11, 1908 – August 28, 1994) served as Bishop of Pittsburgh from 1969 to 1983.

John Bradshaw Butler (November 12, 1927 – May 11, 2013) was an American football cornerback for the Pittsburgh Steelers of the National Football League (NFL).

Brothers John E. ("Jack") Biddle (1872–1902) and Edward C. ("Ed") Biddle (1876–1902) were condemned prisoners who escaped from the Allegheny County Jail in Pittsburgh, Pennsylvania using tools and weapons supplied to them by the warden's wife, Kate Soffel.

There is one quick story I want to share with you about the Calvary Cemetery. One evening, a couple of friends and I walked to theend of Kilbourne Street where it meets Tesla Way. Tesla Way runs with the cemetery. As intrigued kids, we decided to crawl under the fence to get into the cemetery. Walking around in the dark we came upon a bearded man in a black gown sitting on a concrete bench with his head looking down. Was he a priest or was he the devil? We did not stick around. I ran so fast to get out of the Cemetery, my back was scrapped from the bottom of the fence. Some things you never forget.

Each year the VFW, American Legion and local community holds a Memorial Day service to honor our country's fallen military menand women. Days before Memorial Day, the proud people of the surrounding area will place 14,000 plus flags on the graves of all the Veterans. Strength and determination equal freedom.
God Bless Our America!

Calvary Cemetery

14

Legend of the Razorback

It was a Saturday morning, and most people were asleep.
My cousins Lynda, Bobby and I decided on a trip to see the "Legend"
nicknamed the "Big Boy."

"The great pig folklore." Did this exist or was it just a myth?
Not yet dusty in the early morning dew, the road to the farm was wooded
with dark hues.
Our trek through the hills with the giant oak and sycamore trees, draped
over the land like the story of a little boy and girl set in medieval
Germany.
Crossing our favorite pond with lizards, frogs and turtles. Crawling
under multi-floral rose, we finally reached the top of the plateau.
Fruit filled trees enveloped across the land. Blackberries, cherries,
peaches and pears. Let's not forget the delicious red apples to share.

Arriving at the farm on top of the sunlit prairie, a gentle breeze drifted
with a mint smell a little like rosemary.
All of a sudden, a Doberman came running.
Frozen in our tracks, sweat pouring off our backs.
Inches from my feet, salvia spewing from his teeth.
I hear a whistle and a yell, Gina! Gina! She stopped in her tracks.
The dog turns a 180 degrees and retreats.

Greeted by a black man. Polite and friendly. He introduced himself
rather gently. His name Charlie.
Lynda and I asked him if we could tour the farm.
Rumors of a large boar named Big Boy, we wanted to make sure.

His children came running with smiles from ear to ear.
Donna and Doll were their names and they both ran like a deer.
When they invited us onto their farm,
we chased the chickens, the ducks, and played without harm.
An hour or so later we had lunch.
A favorite kids meal, cheese sandwiches and cherry punch.

After lunch our trek becomes real.
Finally, finally the truth is revealed.
Big Boy! Big Boy! Where is the king?
The minds indeed, for we hope to bring.

Come on! Come on! Donna shouted out.
We sprinted to the pen, past the roster and his hen.
Oh my gosh. The thoughts in our head.
We were quick and slick, up the hill we sped.

In no time at all we arrived at the pen.
We hear the sounds of snorting and slopping again and again.
We climbed to the top of a wood plank fence.
What my eyes did see. I could not believe.
I felt like peeing my pants.
It was BIG BOY! A gigantic boar.
A Volkswagen Bug on all fours.

Doll blurts out. "Lets ride."
We all shout. "What!"
"Come on! Don't be afraid. Let's ride."

With enough nerve we jumped on Big Boy,
and road him like a bundle of joy.
After the fun and games it was time to leave.
What a tremendous day. Who would believe?

Now we can go home and tell the true story about Big Boy,
the Real McCoy.

Charlie Johnson with Big Boy

As told by Donna Johnson.

We moved to Hazelwood in 1967. My dad bought the property from a man named "Banks." I was 7 years old. There was at that time a young Doberman named Gina. Gina belonged to Banks but he didn't want her anymore. The dog was mean as hell. Well, being a daring child, I was talking to Gina from afar. If she were my friend, I would not let anyone harm her. Somehow Gina understood my love for animals. One day she went into a seizure, and I was able to calm her down. Before you know it, I was walking out of the barn with her. Gina became my pet. Dad could not believe it.

My dad was originally from Alabama, and he wanted more animals for the farm. We had chickens, ducks, horses, one pony and yes pigs. So many in which they all had names like Big Boy, Ethel, Princess, Print Pig. "Why did the farm close?" I believe it was political or possibly, another adverse situation during those times. Needless to say, we moved down to where my parent's owned property on Elizabeth Street. One day someone burned down our house, killed our dog and caught him on fire. They hurt our pony that was going to another farm. Unfortunately, that is why we have few pictures to show.

If it were up to me, I would have lived at the farm my entire life. It was a magical place like the Wizard of Oz. When Dorothy stepped out the door, everything was beautiful. But after we moved everything turned out to be different. Maybe it was us who was the magic.

Charlie Johnson, Wife Madge Johnson. Brothers—James, Weldon (Nick), Charles (Ray), Michael (Mike). Sisters—Elaine (Doll), Donna, Lisa (Dee) and Rosetta (Rose). All Johnson's.

15

B-25 Ghost Bomber

On January 30, 1956, an Airforce (Air National Guard) B-25 Mitchel bomber departed Nellis Airforce Base in Nevada. The purpose of the flight was to pick up aircraft parts and delivery of two passengers at the Olmsted Airforce Base in Pennsylvania. The Olmsted Airforce Base was located where the Harrisburg International Airport is today, in Middletown, Pennsylvania, nine miles southeast of Harrisburg. In September 1917, the Heinz Pickle farm was replaced with an Army warehouse. Planes began to come and go to deliver and receive supplies.

The crew consisted of Major William L. Dotson, Pilot. Captain John F. Jamieson, Pilot. Captain Steve W. Tobak, Pilot. Staff Sergeant Walter E. Soocey, Crew Chief, and Airman Second Class Charles L. Smith, Crew Chief. Captain J.F. Ingraham and Master Sergeant Alfred J. Alleman were listed as the passengers.

The B-25 departed Nellis Airforce Base at 6:15 p.m. EST. and arrived at Tinker Airforce Base, Oklahoma at 10:21 p.m. EST. The crew decided to RON-Remain Over Night at Tinker Base in view of ice and snow on the runways at Selfridge. Before the next point of destination, a new right brake assembly and left outboard brake assembly were replaced. The B-25 was refueled, and the flight resumed at 8:53 a.m. EST. January 31, 1956. At approximately 1:13 p.m. EST. the crew arrived at Selfridge Airforce in Harrison Township, Michigan. "The Selfridge Field was one of 32 camps established after World War I." Upon arrival at Selfridge, notification was received that they would have to wait 3 hours before refueling the B-25.

The crew decided to continue on without refueling the aircraft. The B-25 had 375 gallons of fuel, this represented approximately 3 hours of flight time. Olmsted Airforce Base was 1 hour and 40 minutes total flight time, more than enough fuel was available to reach the Base. The aircraft departed Selfridge at 2:43 p.m. EST. with Major Dotson as pilot and Captain Jamieson as co-pilot. Captain Tabak remained at Selfridge. The flight proceeded at 7000 feet under IFR "Instrument Flight Rules" conditions heading to Olmsted. Vectoring (position reports) were given by Captain Jamieson at various cities including Butler Pa.

At approximately 31 nautical miles east of Greater Pittsburgh Airport, an unusual amount of fuel dropped in all tanks was indicated. With only 120 gallons of fuel, the B-25 was directed to land at Greater Pittsburgh Airport. While descending, it was noted that the fuel quantity was dropping rapidly and at this time the wing tanks were indicating empty. The main tanks had approximately 80 gallons of fuel remaining. After descending to 3000 feet, the pilot was advised to change course to avoid a large housing area. The fuel was decreasing at an abnormal rate, and it was decided to head for Allegheny County Airport. Shortly after, at 4:11 p.m. EST. the engines ceased operating at 3000 feet. The Monongahela River was spotted, and it was decided to make an emergency landing in the river. Captain Jamieson transmitted "Mayday" on the intercom which was heard at the Allegheny County Tower.

Major Dotson lowered the flaps and completed a successful gear up landing on the water. Eyewitnesses saw the bomber glide over the Homestead High Level Bridge and splash-land near the Glenwood Bridge in Hays. Everyone on the plane survived the crash-landing and were able to climb up to the upper area of the aircraft as it drifted downstream. Reports show that the plane stayed afloat for 10-15 minutes, but as it began to sink, the crew members, who could all swim, either swam for a log floating by or set out for the shore. Sadly, two members sunk beneath the frigid river water, most likely succumbing to hypothermia. The bodies of Capt. Jean Ingraham and Staff Sgt. Walter Soocey were not found for months later.

What happened over the next two weeks fueled one of Pittsburgh's greatest unsolved mysteries... **What became of the B-25 bomber?** In the ensuing hours, a Coast Guard cutter – the Forsythia – snagged a wing of the submerged plane while dragging its anchor. But the line slipped, and the B-25 slid to its watery grave, never to be seen again. The search efforts by the U.S. Coast Guard and the Army Corps of Engineers continued for 14 days but the bomber was never recovered. Theories about the plane's disappearance are plentiful and are still discussed throughout Pittsburgh.

Original Filmet/M.Kambic work

Filmet/M. Kambic/D. Houk/Ulric/GalerieGlobien/B25 Recovery Group

The B-25 medium bomber was one of America's most famous airplanes of WW II. It was used by General Doolittle for the Tokyo Raid on April 18, 1942. Although the airplane was originally intended for level bombing from medium altitudes, it was used extensively in the Pacific area for bombing Japanese airfields from treetop level and for strafing and skip bombing enemy shipping. More than 9,800 B-25s were built during WW II.

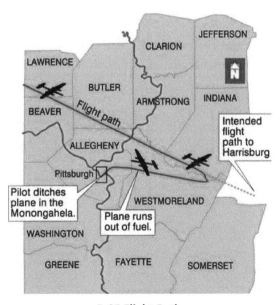

B-25 Flight Path

B-25 DITCHING

A—DITCHING

B—SINKING SITE

B1—INGRAHM DISSAPEARED

E—APPROXIMATE AIRCRAFT

B2—LEEVAN RESCUED

C—SOCCEY DISSAPEARED

D—DOTSON RESCUED, JAMISON RESCUED, SMITH RESCUED

ALL LOCATIONS APPROXIMATE

How does a 15-foot high B-25 bomber go missing in a 20-foot deep river? Several once-classified documents have helped to shed light on the B-25's accident, but its final resting place is still unknown.

Conspiracy theories suggest the bomber carried dangerous or mysterious cargo and that the U.S. military secretly recovered the plane's wreckage overnight after the crash landing to hide its true contents.

Some believe the B-25 bomber may have been carrying a nuclear weapon or even a UFO from Area 51 near Las Vegas.

Others cling to cover-up myths that range from the plane carrying Soviet agents, Howard Hughes and Las Vegas show girls destined to entertain senators in Washington, D.C.

In recent years, a team of volunteers known as the B-25 Recovery Group worked with the Heinz History Center with the hopes of locating the lost plane.

In 1995, the B-25 Recovery Group was led by the late **John Uldrich**, military historian and CEO of a Minneapolis-Shanghai-based marketing consultancy firm. **Bob Shema,** who brings over **50** years of experience to the B-25 recovery project that includes an in-depth understanding of the Monongahela River and the river's complex environment and the application of side and sector scan sonar in littoral settings and a unique understanding when man, machine and the river meet.

Bob's role within the group is that of Operations Director.

His responsibilities include the planning and scheduling of all river-borne activities.

Additionally, Bob is responsible for the acquisition and use of specialized equipment, safety of operations while on the water and post mission research activities. Among his personal accomplishments, Bob Shema is a USCG licensed Captain and has received recognition by the United States Coast Guard for his work in navigation safety.

Steve Byers, the founder and owner of Sennex Corporation. Mr. Byers is currently involved in the Nationwide expansion of Sennex's computer training division, Computer Solutions Today. **Richard Eugene Cole**, (Honorable Member) lieutenant colonel of the United States Airforce was the last survivor in the Doolittle Raids who passed away in 2020.

Matt Pundzak, Senior Staff Engineer for Intel-Data, Incorporated, a Virginia-based firm specializing in systems engineering support to government.

A retired Air Force Intelligence Officer, Matt brings twenty years of "hands on" military experience and technical insight to the team. His experience within the military and government includes airborne recon-naissance, special operations, national level intelligence collection and the application of technology to the intelligence and information domain.

My wife and I had the privilege to interview **Bob Shema** at my home on August 1, 2021. Bob Shema and the B-25 Recovery Group rejects all conspiracy theories and have spent about 26 years conducting scientific research, including physically searching the river, to identify the location of the missing plane.

Bob explained that a metal detecting magnetometer is the best tool to be use in locating the remains of the bomber. After 65 years of the river being a subject to acid concentrations, and river traffic, Bob believes this non-intrusive sensor has the best chance of locating the B-25 which would now be in a fragile and corroded state. Once the target is located by the magnetometer, selective excavations will be conducted to confirm the bomber's presence. Evidence of the bomber will likely be small samples of metal collected during the excavations. These samples will then be analyzed to confirm that are the same materials originally used in the construction of the aircraft. If evidence exists that the aircraft is intact, an effort may be mounted to recover part or the entire bomber. From the years 1941 to 1978, seven aircraft ditched or crashed intothe three rivers of Pittsburgh. Of the seven, six planes had been recovered. The B-25 sits alone in the fathomless abyss.

The B-25 group has a mixture of engineers, lawyers, military historiansand ex-military members. Bob works with **Richard G. Riley Jr.**

Owner / President of **Marion Hill Associates, Inc.**, a diving company based in New Brighton. Marion Hill Associates consists of Deep air & mixed gas diving, underwater inspections, underwater video, dam inspection and repair, nuclear diving and more.

The airplane was recovered "On August 4, 1996, approximately 6:37p.m. eastern daylight time, an Aerotek, Pitts Special S-1S, N2HT, was destroyed when a wing failed while performing aerobatics at the Three Rivers Regatta, and impacted in the Ohio River in Pittsburgh, Pennsylvania. The certificated commercial pilot/owner received fatal injuries. Visual meteorological conditions prevailed and no flight plan had been filed for the local flight." On August 6, the Salvage crew raised the wreckage of the stunt plane from the Ohio River and found the pilot's body inside. Clarence 'Clancy' Speal, 43, from the Pittsburgh suburb of New Alexandria,

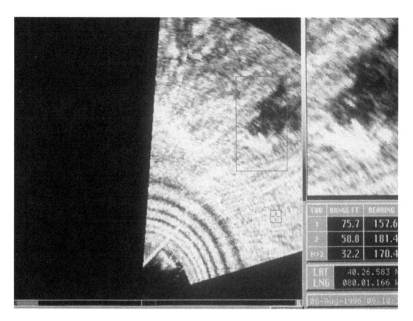

The "Pitts Special" was located with a Side Scan Sonar and then a Sector Scan Sonar to observe the diver and position of aircraft.

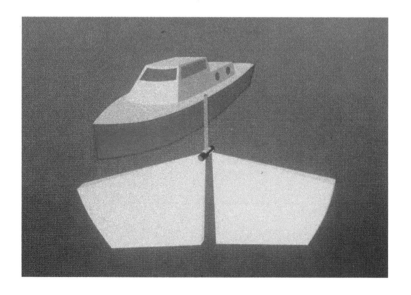

Side Scan Sonar

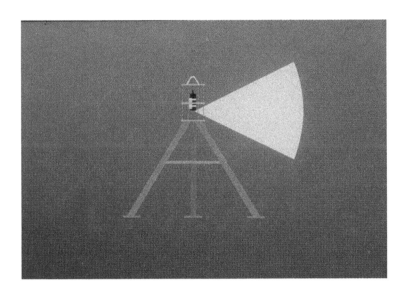

Sector Scan

Bob Shema and the B-25 Recovery Group rejects those conspiracy theories and have spent about 26 years collecting scientific research, including physically probing the river, to identify the location of the missing plane. Bob believes the remnants of the B-25 can be found buried in about 15 feet of silt, below 32 feet of water and 150 feet from the riverbank in a place called "Bird's Landing," about a mile down the river from the Glenwood Bridge. The plane slipped into a hole that Dravo Corp. dug in the early 1950s to obtain fill material for mooring cells that J&L Steel built downriver.

16

Some Other Experiences

Former Worldwide Wrestling Federation (WWWF) star passed away February 26, 2021 in Pittsburgh, Pa. **Mr. Johnny De Fazio** was a long time personality in Pittsburgh. He wrestled from the early 1960's until the mid 1980's.

Not only was John a wrestler, but he was also a valued public servant in the community. John served as a union leader for the US Steelworkers and a county councilman for Allegheny County. He eventually became council president until 2019.

At one time he had his office behind the 5 and 10 store, at Flowers and Second Avenue. Many times, I would see him going in and out of his office dressed in a suit and tie. One glance at Mr. De Fazio would lead to a double take. Most times I would see him wearing short black tight wrestling pants.

John was a bipartisan leader of council, and a teacher for new members. He encouraged unity among the council and focused on improving the quality of living for the people.

One historical building known as the Speck Block building is situated at Second Avenue and Hazelwood Avenue. Built in 1886 by laborers from Homestead Pa, this building covered half the block and is very well known in the community. In the 1930's it was a cigar store called the "Smoke Dry Slitz Stogies." Over the years the building is well known for many great food shops. Currently the building houses Jozsa's Corner Hungarian Restaurant. The late Freda Pyrek Kish prepared German-Italian style hoagies until the mid-1980s. Today the restaurant is owned and operated by a local celebrity named Alex Bodnar. Bodnar was featured on the Travel Channel, "No Reservations" and WQED's "What Makes Pittsburgh." A documentary.

Speck Block Building
Built 1886

There was an Olympic hero that hailed from Hazelwood. **Herb Douglas** won a bronze medal in the long jump at the 1948 Olympic games at Wembley Stadium in London, England. Douglas attended Gladstone Elementary School and Gladstone Junior High School. As a teenager, he idolized Jesse Owens' performance in the 1936 Olympics. He was playing football and running track when he graduated from Allderdice High School. Attending the University of Pittsburgh, Douglas won three collegiate titles in the long jump. He earned his B.S. degree from the University of Pittsburgh in 1948.

A mural commemorating his bronze medal jump is painted, newspaper-style, on the corner of Second Avenue and Tecumseh Street in his native Hazelwood. Douglas became a successful businessman in the alcohol industry. He was one of the first African American vice presidents of any North American company.

Another famous person from Hazelwood was **Dave 'Rooster' Fleming.** Dave is honored in the Western Pennsylvania Sports Hall of Fame and the Minor Pro Football Hall of Fame. In 1963 and 1964, he was on the reserve squad for the Pittsburgh Steelers, lining up with the likes of Bill Nelsen, Tom "The Bomb" Tracy, Myron Pottios and a rookie named Andy Russell. When the Steelers cut Fleming, he went to train-ing camp with the New York Jets. That's where he roomed with Namath,the superstar quarterback from Beaver Falls. O'Brien told the tale of Broadway Joe and Rooster hurdling the turnstiles together to sneak into the World's Fair in Flushing, N.Y. Rooster played 10 seasons in the CFL,winning three Grey Cup championships with the Hamilton Tiger-Cats. It was said that Dave Fleming fought professional wrestling legend Bruno Sammartino in a backstage brawl. Fleming was known as a devoted husband and father. He married his high school sweetheart, Susan, who suffered from multiple sclerosis for 47 years and was a paraplegic for 35 years before her death in 2018.

Marguerite "Dolly" Pearson (Tesseine) (September 6, 1932 – January 4, 2005) was a utility player who played in The All-American Girls Professional Baseball League. The AAGPBL flourished in the 1940s when Major League Baseball was put on hold because of World War II. The league was created in 1943 by the Chicago Cubs owner Philip K. Wrigley. In its twelve years of history, the AAGPBL had over 600 women athletes play professional baseball.

Born in Pittsburgh, a neighborhood of Hazelwood, Dolly played seven years in the league. During her tenure, Dolly played for seven different clubs around the league. She played in all positions except catcher before becoming a regular shortstop.

Dolly was the daughter of William and Retha (Hayes) Pearson. She attended Allderdice High School. She would play organized baseball with the boys and gained a solid reputation. An AAGPBL scout caught wind, and signed Pearson at the age of 15, the youngest player ever to play in the league. On the last day of her rookie season, Pearson celebrated her16th birthday. To everybody's surprise, because 16 was the minimum age according to the rules, she had played illegally for one season. Once the league folded, Dolly settled in Grand Rapids, Michigan for 15 years before moving to Mount Pleasant, Michigan. She started playing slow-pitch softball until the age of 65.

Dolly is part of "Women in Baseball" an honor displayed at the Baseball Hall of Fame in Cooperstown New York.

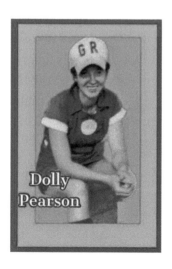

Fredrick August Wilson Kittel Jr. known as August Wilson was an American playwright born in the Hill District on April 27, 1945. August was a German and African American decent. In the 1950's his family moved to Hazelwood where they faced racial hostilities. Wilson's life was influenced by Malcolm X and his plays showed these historic advents in time. His first play "Pittsburgh Cycle" was about growing up in the Hill District during these trying times. His Notable awards were very impressive. Pulitzer Prize for Drama (1987, 1990), Whiting Award (1986), Heinz Award in the arts and Humanities (2004). August Wilson passed away on October 2, 2005. His resting place is at the Greenwood Cemetery in Pittsburgh, Pa.

August Wilson

Herb Douglas 1948 Summer Olympics

Dave Fleming

Jim O'Brien, Pittsburgh sports author, lived his first five years at 5413 Sunnyside Street. He lived in a row house as many Hazelwood residents did at the time. It was said Jim's father was born on a couch in that house. His family moved to the adjoining Almeda Street later on. The O'Briens lived on one side of a duplex house on Almeda Street, and the Burns family lived next door. His mother, Mary Burns, lived in that house as a young woman. His father and mother eventually courted one another. It was a story like "Ozzie and Harriet." The duplex house is still standing, and people still reside there.

Jim is on the advisory board for the Western Pennsylvania Sports Museum at the Heinz History Center in Pittsburgh and has been inducted into the Western Chapter of the Pennsylvania Sports Hall of Fame. He was given the Bob Prince Award for his journalism efforts and the David L. Lawrence Award for "promoting Pittsburgh in a positive manner on a national level" from Vectors. He was cited as a "Legend" by the Pittsburgh chapter of the Italian American Sports Hall of Fame. Jim was the first Pittsburgher to be inducted into the U. S. Basketball Writers Association Hall of Fame at ceremonies at the Regency Hyatt in New Orleans.

Mr. O'Brien also spoke of cultural diversity as a "common heritage of humanity" and respect. Each race encompassed a multitude of different ethnic groups due to the large part of immigrant migration at the height of the industrial revolution. Learning about other cultures helped us understand different perspectives within our town and city. Jim told of his improvising mind to form sport teams as a youth, building ballfields in vacant lots and raised money to purchase T-shirts for his team. As a son of Hazelwood, he has made the community proud.

Sister Catherine "Cathy" Cesnik was a Nun and English / Drama teacher at the former all-girls Archbishop Keough High School in Baltimore, Maryland. Sister Cathy is originally from Lawrenceville, Pa. Approximately 15 minutes (5 miles) north of Hazelwood. On November 7, 1969, Cathy disappeared from her Baltimore apartment. Her body was later discovered on January 3, 1970, near a garbage dump in Lansdowne, Maryland by a hunter and his son. The autopsy determined that she was murdered from a blunt force to the head. As of today, her murder still remains a mystery and is the basis for the Netflix documentary series Called " The Keepers."
Sister Catherine is buried at Saint Mary's Cemetery, Sharpsburg, Pennsylvania. She was only 26 years old.

A few years ago, my cousin Maggie gave me directions to the cemetery. When I saw Sister's grave I broke down. Her tombstone was dirty and worn. Something happened to me that day. I started having nightmares and couldn't sleep for weeks. One day I decided to place some flowers on her grave. I bought a special cleaner and sealer for her stone. I cleaned, sealed and placed flowers around her stone. The nightmares have been going away. Every couple months I will clean and place fresh flowers around her stone. My heart breaks for this poor woman.

Saint Anthony's Chapel on Troy Hill was built in 1880 by Father Suitbert Mollinger, who was pastor at the Most Holy Name of Jesus Parrish. Suibert Mollinger was educated in Amsterdam and studied medicine in Naples, Rome, Genoa and later attended seminary in Ghent. He formed an alliance with American bishops in search for volunteers. In 1854 he traveled to New York, went to Labtrobe and later Ohio. Eleven years later he arrived in Pittsburgh and established several mission parishes. On July 4, 1868, he became pastor of the Most Holy Name of Jesus Parrish.

Saint Anthony's Chapel is home to the largest collection of Christian relics second to the Vatican. Due to his personal financial ability, the chapel and over 5000 relics were his personal property. Father Mollinger was in a position to purchase a large number of relicsthat were both legally and illegally for sale on the open market. In addition to his duty as pastor, Father Mollinger's education as a medical doctor tended to the physical needs of the community. Father Mollinger treated over 325,000 patients in which many claimed miracle healings. Father Mollinger passed away on 15 Jun 1892 (aged 64).

Saint Anthony's Chapel

US Steel Tower

Switch Station

Pittsburgh Railway Company

Glenwood B&O Railroad Bridge

Switch Station

Shocking Truth

At The Cliffs

The US and many other countries around the world are witnessing a rise in tent encampments. Tent cities have been on the rise in almost every state since 2016. In the United States, 190,000 people were homeless on any given night. The stereotypical image of a person who is homeless is thought to be a drug addict or alcohol user. Many people fall into homelessness because of job loss, domestic violence, divorce, evictions and health issues. As a result, from these issues, many people fall into drug addiction, alcohol and mental obstacles. Based on a survey, 98% of the homeless said that they would move into a safe and affordable house if available. Many churches and non-profit organizations address homelessness by providing basic needs, such as food and shelter, but do little to help find homes. Many cities do not have adequate resources nor the plans to address the problem, which continues to increase.

Nansen Street Boardwalk

Walking Bridge from Lytle Street

Glenwood Bridge

Calvary Cemetery

Rutherglen St. Footbridge

Hazelwood Fire Station

Flowers Avenue

Obrien Hall a legitimate social club for members of AA "Alcoholics Anonymous." Meetings, gatherings, someplace to go.

John D. O'Connor & Son Funeral Home

Est: 1927

Second Avenue

J & L Art Work

Proud People of Hazelwood

Hazelwood Clean Up

Second Avenue Head Start

The Old 5 & 10

University of Pittsburgh

Cathedral of Learning

J & L Steel

The Memories

SECOND AVENUE

Following Pittsburgh's substantial decline, Hazelwood suffered a compelling population loss and a business withdrawal as a result of the steel industry shutting down in 1997. However, in 2002, the 178 acre uninhabited site was purchased by Almono Lp corporation marking the beginning of a new aera for Hazelwood. Since then, the community has organized a program to reinvest and revitalize their town to move forward.

Twenty three years later, a master plan and public input will begin for the restoration of the riverfront land, comprising 21 acres and extending 1.3 miles alone the Monongahela river.

The neighborhood is bursting for opportunities to regenerate a cultural creativity for the town and the city of Pittsburgh. Hazelwood residents shall play a key role in shaping the growth for the community.

The Global Silicon Valley Labs which connect startups with investors and corporations through a global online platform will establish its next innovative hub at Hazelwood Green. They have supported startups in more than 100 countries and presented outstanding results. GSV labs signed a long-term lease in developing the Almono's 178-acre site along the Monongahela River. The company expects to locate there in the second quarter of 2021.

Hazelwood Green released its long-range plan with complete streets and bike lanes. Its Mill 19 building opened in 2020 and eventually the property will have offices, research and development, light manufacturing, retail, housing, public green spaces and trails. Carnegie Mellon University's Advanced Robotics for Manufacturing and Catalyst Connection will be the first tenants. The Autonomous vehicle company Aptiv is expected to locate in Mill 19.

Glistening streetlights, trees and bus islands outline the new Lytle Street, which intersects with Hazelwood Avenue and takes drivers, bicyclists or pedestrians on protected sidewalks and bike routes toward Mill 19. Eventually, the new stretch of Lytle Street will connect to the existing Lytle Street, migrating to nearby streets lined with houses.

Acknowledgments

Writing a book is harder than I ever thought and more rewarding than I could have ever imagined. None of this would have been possible without my wife, **Anna Marie**. She has tolerated my tension, anxiety and stressful situations. Anna Marie has stood by me during every struggle and all my successes. She sustained me in ways that I never knew that Ineeded, especially with my seizure activity.

To my kids**, Brooke Riley**, son-in-law **Gwynn Riley**, **Patrick Bonner**, daughter-in-law **Courtney Bonner** and my grandkids **Briar Bonner** and **Coraline Bonner**. You all have made me stronger, better and more fulfilled than I could have ever imagined. I love you all.

Thank you to my cousin **Maggie Reider** for proof reading and her positive influence for me to keep me going.

An additional thanks to **Denis Perris (DeDe)** owner of the **Lytle Café** and her daughters, **Michelle Parris Auberzinshy, Camille Parris Clifford, and Denise Parris Provident (Niecy)** for their great advice.

Special thanks to Sports Author **Jim O'Brien** for allowing me to interview him and share his experiences growing up in Hazelwood.

Thank you, Donna Johnson Torres, for sharing her story living on the farm where Big Boy was.

Thank you, Ja Quay**, Edward Carter** and the **Hazelwood Historical Society** for allowing me to share their old Photo's.

I appreciate **Bernadette DiPietro** for her Photos of J&L steel mill.

Thanks to **Fabien** and **Lisanne Moreau,** owners **of La Gourmandine Bakery**. Thanks to **Aqua Roseanne** Meloy, employee with La Gourmandine Bakery.

Thanks to **Dianne Shenk**, owner of **Dylamato's Market** for her wonderful story.

Thanks to **Eddie Provident** for a great cover design.

Thank you, Jeanette Davis, for sending me a photo of hergreat-grandfather on Dido Street.

Thanks to my classmates from Saint Stephen's school, **Ed Jenkins, Cathy DiThomas Farkal, David King, David North, Joe Szewcow, Renee Marino** for sharing their memories.

Thanks to my Cousins **Lynda M. Weaver**, **Bobby Coombs**, **Valerie Ondruseck, Bunny Dillion Murray** for their stories.
Thank you, Eddie Cerillie, for all the connections.
Thanks to **Kathy Turek Merante**, **Carol Musser Reffner**, **Jill Evey Wanzie**, **Judeen Wayman** for support in my venture.

Thanks to the patrons of the "**Lytle Café**" **John Gergacs, John Kish, Bobby Perris, Floyd Clawson, Fritz Phillips** and **Harry Bolton**.

Thanks to **Marie-Lou Chatel**—-from Belgium for her photo on Page 166

Thanks to **Robert Shema who Leads the Way in Research of River Mystery.** I had a great privilege to have Bob at my home and interview him and to supply me with the great pictures.

Thanks to all from Hazelwood, Saint Stephen's School, Bethel Park and Canonsburg. Thanks to my Karate students for handling my stress.